Flyi

Greg McMillan

Manor House Publishing

Library and Archives Canada
Cataloguing in Publication

McMillan, Greg, 1952-
    Flying high : Hamilton's airport and economy soar to
new heights / Greg McMillan.

ISBN 978-1-897453-01-8

    1. John C. Munro Hamilton International Airport--History.
2. Airports--Economic aspects--Ontario--Hamilton. 3. Hamilton
(Ont.)--Economic conditions. 4. Business enterprises--Ontario--
Hamilton.
I. Title.
HE9797.5.C32H34 2007   387.7'360971352
 C2007-905316-5

Cover photo courtesy: Westjet

Published by Manor House Publishing Inc.
4522 Cottingham Crescent, Ancaster, Ontario, Canada, L9G 3V6
905-648-2193.... Fax: 905-648-8369
www.manor-house.biz

We acknowledge the financial support of the Government of
Canada through the Book Publishing Industry Development
Program (BPIDP) for our publishing activities.

About the photography: All photos appearing in Flying High
– with the exception of the front cover, Bick Financial Security,
Dr. Roland Estrabillo, Ken Lindsay and Ron Foxcroft – were
crafted by D'Arcy McNeil and Angela DeSalvo of Empirical
Photographic Arts (www.empiricalphotographicarts.com),
telephone 519.752.1158, in Brantford, Ontario.

For Richard and Audrey McMillan, my parents, who cannot be thanked enough for continuing to provide life-long support and love. Their encouragement to "follow your dreams" has enabled me – with a clear conscience – to truly live life. Everyone should be so fortunate.

Foreword

"Flying High" is indeed an appropriate title for a book focusing on Hamilton's international airport.

As you're about to read, Hamilton has benefited tremendously from the growth of the airport in the 10 years since TradePort assumed management. And we believe the best is yet to come.

Hamilton is now connected by air to the rest of Canada, North America and the world. That's a remarkable achievement. It's hard to believe that just 10 years ago only 16,000 passengers used the facility and the number of destinations was limited to two.

Now, more than 600,000 business and pleasure travelers fly from Hamilton on Canada's two leading air carriers, WestJet and Air Canada, non-stop to Vancouver, Calgary, Edmonton, Winnipeg, Ottawa, Montreal, Moncton, Halifax, Orlando and several sun destinations with convenient connections to destinations throughout the United States and Europe.

Flyglobespan, a popular low-cost carrier in the United Kingdom, commenced service in May 2007, from Hamilton International to 13 destinations in the U.K. and Ireland.

In fact, a record number of destinations were being served from Hamilton in 2007. As the word of this convenience spreads, more and more passengers will take advantage of the convenience of Hamilton International. And please consider the following points:
• Hamilton Airport is now the site of approximately 1,700

jobs as it has grown to become Canada's largest dedicated cargo hub. 10 years ago the facility only provided a handful of jobs, and today activity at the airport contributes over $400 million to the economy. Some industry observers suggest we could have as many as 50,000 airport and airport-related jobs over the next 25 years.

• In 1996 and for many years previously, the taxpayers of Hamilton were asked to subsidize the operations of the airport to the tune of $1 million per year. Since TradePort assumed management the subsidies have ended, saving Hamilton taxpayers approximately $10 million over the course of 10 years of transparent management.

• TradePort and airport tenants have invested approximately $120 million in construction and other capital projects since TradePort assumed management. Most of that money was spent on local labour and suppliers, and all investments vest to Hamilton taxpayers at the end of TradePort's lease.

The future of John C Munro Hamilton International Airport is even brighter. We have an immediate passenger catchment area of 2.3 million people who increasingly find it to their advantage to avoid the gridlock of Pearson by flying from Hamilton.

With increased fuel and other cost pressures on the airline industry, more and more carriers are expressing interest in Hamilton, where a lower airport cost structure and quick aircraft turnaround allow for significantly lower operating costs.

At what is a really positive juncture in the history of Hamilton Airport, it is important everyone know TradePort is committed to working in close cooperation with the owners of the airport — the City of Hamilton, and by extension with the taxpayers of Hamilton. We enjoy an excellent working relationship with City staff and the community at large and we intend to build on that relationship for our mutual benefit in the future.

Ten years into our 40-year lease agreement, an independent audit, conducted by Grant Thornton, confirms TradePort has invested $45 million into the airport. It further shows the shareholders re-invested all earnings, plus an additional $10 million, back into airport development, while spending $5 million on marketing. Simply put, the audit confirms the tremendous investment that has been made into the airport and the Hamilton community.

We're proud of our record and our dedicated people who have helped make our achievements possible.

We believe the decades to come will bring further growth and prosperity to our community as our airport further develops its role as Hamilton's economic engine. With this growth will come more flights, more jobs, more investments and more opportunities to explore the open skies.

We have a promising future before us and we are, in every sense of the phrase, flying high.

Richard Koroscil, President/CEO, Hamilton International

About the Author

Greg McMillan has come full circle: Brantford, Ontario to Brantford Ontario, travelling many diverse roads in between.

Born and raised in the Telephone City, he went on to journalism school, and got his first newspaper job as Sports Editor of the Dundas Valley Journal.

From there it was a quick hop to the Hamilton Spectator as a freelance sports reporter/photographer, then several months as a reporter/photographer at the Stratford Beacon Herald before returning to The Spectator as a "two-way man" at the Grimsby Bureau.

He spent 10 years at The Spec, moving about in such roles as Assistant District Editor, Layout Editor, Assistant Sports Editor and Pop Music Critic. He raised his son David – now a professional golfer based in San Antonio, Texas – and actively participated as a coach and manager in minor hockey and lacrosse.

Then it was on to the Globe and Mail in Toronto, where he served as editorial liaison for a massive redesign project, before moving on there to positions as Graphics Editor and Art Director.

During that time, he also started a marketing/publishing company that, among other things, produced advertorial sections for the Globe, with clients such as the Toronto Raptors and IBM.

Next stop was the Dominican Republic, where he planned to write a reality-based book – before the world had ever heard of the concept of the TV series Survivor – away from the tourist enclaves. That project did not exactly turn out as he had originally envisioned, however, and he ended up staying on, being exposed to much more than he had originally bargained for.

He started an English/Spanish computer school up in the mountains of Jarabacoa with students ranging in age from four up to 58, most of them totally illiterate in both languages. Among several other ventures, he also served as student advisor for the first year of the United Nations Association of the Dominican Republic. However, those experiences were merely the tip of the iceberg – there are many other off-the-beaten-track stories to tell.

Now he's back in Brantford, where it all started, and – thanks to technology – continues to write and pursue far-flung journalism-related and import/export endeavours. He sees Canada in a totally different light these days – years in a developing country will do that to you – and is able to savor family moments and care for his daughter who was born in the Dominican Republic.

He's an Associate Senior Writing/Communications Strategist at C2E Consulting in Toronto, where he's lauded as "one of the most widely talented and experienced editorial resources in the Canadian market, with over three decades of experience in writing, editing, art direction and layout."

Greg is also the owner of a website, www. therealdominican.com He plays harmonica and loves the blues and bachata, which he calls the Dominican blues.

His first book was entitled A Chronicle of Images: The History of Relations between Canada and the Dominican Republic and published in English, Spanish and French. It was commissioned by the Canadian ambassador to the Dominican Republic.

Flying High takes Greg back to his roots in many ways, and now he looks forward to encountering other challenges and inspirations to embrace on the next bend in the road.

Acknowledgements

I am grateful to publisher/editor Michael Davie for collaborating with me on this project. He was extremely helpful and guided me through any rough spots along the way. He also contributed several business profiles that nicely complemented *Flying High*.

Richard Koroscil, President/CEO of Hamilton International Airport, and Ron Foxcroft, chairman of TradePort International Corporation, founder of Fox 40 International and chairman and CEO of Fluke Transportation Group Ltd. were both extremely responsive and helped put many business aspects into perspective.

At the Canadian Warplane Heritage Museum, my thanks go out to veteran tour guide Bill Tourtel, a natural-born storyteller, and Robin Hill, who patiently responded to my every query.

John Dolbec from the Hamilton Chamber of Commerce and Margaret Houghton of the Hamilton Public Library were others who provided immediate assistance and insight when called upon.

D'Arcy McNeil and Angela DeSalvo of Empirical Photographic Arts (www.empiricalphotographicarts.com), in Brantford, Ontario, deserve very special thanks as they did much more than contribute creative and inspired photography for this book. They were my sounding boards and helped sustain me with their camaraderie and humour.

And finally, many thanks to my wife, Deyanira, who kept my spirits up through emails and telephone conversations from her home in Santo Domingo, Dominican Republic, where she patiently waits for the processing of her spousal visa so she can join our family in Canada.

Prologue

There is something about the John C. Munro Hamilton International Airport (hi) that just seems to bring people together, often from many diverse starting points, all eventually ending up at the same place – you guessed it – the airport in Mount Hope.

In preparing this book, I continually ran into this situation. Everyone I interviewed had a personal story or a favourite recollection about their experience with the airport.

Whether it was John Dolbec, Chief Executive Officer for the Hamilton Chamber of Commerce, my brother Duncan, a golf course superintendent in Calgary, popular 81-year-old tour guide Bill Tourtel at the Hamilton Warplane Heritage Museum, or Ron Foxcroft, inventor of the Fox-40 whistle and Chairman of airport manager TradePort, everyone raved about the airport as a people place, a place that was always a pleasure to visit, whether 40 years ago, or last week.

And I include myself in that group. During my research, I recalled that I had written several articles about the old Hamilton International Airshow back in the 1970s when I was a cub reporter for the Hamilton Spectator working out of the Grimsby Bureau.

So, with a little investigation, I contacted the library at the Hamilton Spectator. I could not recall the exact dates of the articles, nor their exact content, but was fairly certain they had run sometime after 1975 and before 1980.

Sure enough, Spectator librarian Debbie Haentjens hit paydirt. She did some digging and found articles that were published June 17 and June 19, 1978.

The first story was a first-person account of my flight in a North American B25 Mitchell bomber. It was a setup piece for the weekend airshow which, I reported the following Monday, drew close to 25,000 spectators and broke all existing attendance records.

Our bomber was selected to lead of convoy of World War Two warships, on a formation flight from the Hamilton Civic Airport to Toronto Sick Children's Hospital and back. We circled the CN Tower and then swooped down to within 300 feet of the hospital so that the children could see our assortment of 20-odd warplanes. A dramatic photograph by Andrew Clark, taken from inside the bomber, and showing other warplanes over Toronto, accompanied the article.

The article also pointed out that the airshow, sponsored by the Canadian Warplane Heritage, would "feature everything from Joe Hughes and his wing-walker act to a simulated dogfight between a Japanese Zero and U.S. fighter planes" and that the "majority of the restored planes are at least 30 years old and all immaculately maintained."

The Spectator gave premium coverage to the airshow back then, with two pages dedicated to the event in the Monday edition, with four more of my stories, as well as nine accompanying photos from Spectator Staff photographers John Gast and Bob Chambers.

There were mentions of Oscar Boesch's glider, accompanied by the strains of Born Free; of the impressive formation flying of the Snowbirds, featuring local Canadian Armed Forces pilot John McNamara; and of Sue Parish, the only female pilot in the show, in her Curtis P40 World War II fighter plane.

And then there was 'Crazy' Bob Oakes, the sidekick to aerobatics daredevil Hughes, who had never even been in a small plane until a month before the show. "The first time I was ever up in a small plane, I climbed out on the wing," he told me at the time.

Airshow public relations man at the time, Bob Martin, said: "it was the smoothest show ever staged."

He also said the some of the proceeds would be used to help pay off the Canadian Warplane Heritage hangar at the airport. He said there were 380 people working for the show, an increase of 20 per cent from the previous year, and that Canadian Armed Forces cadets and regional police maintained order.

He said any organizational glitches were minor – fences collapsing and the press tent falling down – but that the setup for food was better than the previous year, and there were no problems with gate crashers and none of the aircraft experienced any technical troubles.

"It was family fare all the way," I wrote. "Good-natured and informative announcers tied the shows together with their running commentary and cameras were continually clicking."

Said eight-year-old Roger Croy of Lake Street, St. Catharines: "I liked it all. I'd like to come again."

Alas, those days are long gone; insurance costs after 9/11 finally led to the demise of the airshow. Thankfully, the memories linger. Now it is time for new stories and a new history to be written.

One thing is certain: the John C. Munro Hamilton International Airport is still Flying High.

A Word from the Publisher

Greg McMillan offers an informative, personal, insightful look at an important Canadian International airport and its impact on the surrounding Hamilton community and beyond.

In-depth interviews and thought-provoking anecdotes punctuate McMillan's prose as he takes us inside the inner workings of this remarkable facility, with commentary from those who manage and operate John C. Munro Hamilton International Airport.

McMillan also takes us inside the airport's on-site Canadian Warplane Heritage Museum, which houses several unique aircraft and hundreds of exhibits.
He also visits various tenants comprising the airport family, including JetPort, the executive business flight service owned by Ron Joyce, co-founder of Tim Hortons.

As John Dolbec of the Hamilton Chamber of Commerce relates, the airport has had an impressive positive impact on the Hamilton community.

The entire economy has benefited. The financial services sector has flourished with the airport's proven ability to attract more people into the Hamilton region, and the medical sector has also grown with physical expansions and rising patient loads.

McMillan combines skilled story-telling with insightful observations and intriguing data in this information-packed look at an airport rich with potential.

And he conveys the passenger experience of using this unbelievably convenient, quick and easy way to travel across Canada… and around the world.
Informative, engaging: Welcome to *Flying High*.

Michael B. Davie, author, Winning Ways

1

Let's imagine, for a moment, that you are planning a trip. It could be to England, it could be to the Caribbean, it could even be to a destination in Canada.

Only a few years ago, if you lived in the Golden Horseshoe area, pretty well your only option would be to inquire about flights out of Toronto Pearson International Airport.

Right away, you had a sinking feeling. You knew the logistics of flying out of that airport would not be conducive to a smooth, hassle-free experience.

Then, almost overnight it seemed, a better, more relaxing and user-friendly option to the Pearson nightmare availed itself to you – the John C. Munro Hamilton International Airport (hi), located conveniently in Mount Hope, Ontario, just outside Hamilton.

Suddenly, you didn't have to dread the thought of travelling; in fact, you could eagerly anticipate the entire experience. What a switch!

Ask anyone who has flown out of Hamilton International Airport (hi) and you generally get the same kinds of laudatory kudos – whether it be from a business or leisure traveller.

Ron Foxcroft, founder of Fox 40 International and chairman and CEO of Fluke Transportation Group Ltd., based in the Hamilton area, describes, in a nutshell, the differences in the travel options between using Toronto or Hamilton airports.

"From the minute you get in the car to go to Pearson you have apprehension," said Mr. Foxcroft, also the chairman of TradePort International Corporation, which holds a 40-year lease with the City of Hamilton to develop, manage and operate the Hamilton International Airport. "You start with all the gridlock between Hamilton and Toronto. There is no easy, or good, time. You then have a multitude of parking options … all a long way from the terminal and very expensive.

"Then you have the long lineups, and the big crowds. By the time you line up at the counter, go through security and get to your gate, you feel like you have been dragged through the mud by a team of horses… and you have not yet boarded the plane!

"Once you are actually on the plane, the taxi before takeoff seems to take longer than if you flew to Mars or Pluto!"

Contrast that travel snapshot with the Hamilton example, as described by Duncan McMillan, a Brantford, Ontario, native who now lives in Calgary and flies east one or two times a year, for business and for pleasure.

"How enjoyable it is to disembark from the plane [in Hamilton], pick up your luggage promptly and proceed through the exit immediately to the parking lot or passenger pick-up lanes," said Mr. McMillan, a golf course superintendent. "This, in comparison to Pearson, where you disembark, walk for 15 minutes, wait for at least another 15 minutes for your luggage, and then walk for another 10 minutes to get to your parking area or rental car area."

He succinctly explained his dislikes travelling through Pearson: "Too busy, too big, too many terminals." And Hamilton? "Smaller, more compact, more personal, everything in one place."

Both testimonials are music to the ears of Richard Koroscil, President and CEO of Hamilton International (hi),

15

who has seen major strides taken since taking charge four years ago.

"Southern Ontario business and leisure travellers have discovered that flying Hamilton is indeed flying easy," he says. "Hamilton International offers incredible ease of access, is the key factor for everyone who flies from our airport. Offering greater convenience, travellers enjoy reduced wait times, faster check-in, quicker customs clearance, quick aircraft turnaround, shorter walks through the airport's easy-to-navigate terminal, no congestion and convenient low cost parking.

"Hamilton International is positioned to serve the over 2.3-million people who live within a 50-minute drive and 8.4-million people who live within a 90-minute drive of the airport, and is the perfect choice for travellers heading to or departing from Toronto, Niagara and other locations in Southern Ontario."

Mr. Koroscil points out 2006 was a very successful year for Hamilton International Airport (hi) with 527,133 patrons using the facility.

His team is extremely proud of the fact that there are flights to more destinations than ever before and they are continuing to build their route system with new air carrier partnerships. As always, in 2006 customer satisfaction remained high on their list of priorities as they
continually sought to make the experience at hi a memorable one for all parties involved.

They are pleased to report that they are making excellent progress on strategic objectives of extending passenger services out of hi with the announcement of daily services to 13 UK/Ireland destinations commencing in 2007 on flyglobespan as well as increases in existing air carrier services by 50 per cent; increasing air cargo traffic with expansion of the CargoJet program, and outreach at the Air Cargo Forum in Calgary; enhancing revenue opportunities;

promoting regional tourism through marketing partnerships with various tourism partners; and investing in infrastructure and facilities, including the start of the International Arrivals Hall expansion, completion of the Hold Bag Screening (HBS) facility, installation of Common Use Self Service (CUSS) check-in kiosks and updating of the Federal Airport Zoning, in collaboration with the City of Hamilton.

The airport also introduced its airport volunteer program with the "hi ambassadors," launched a "fly free for life" contest, structured a Community Advisory Board and participated in and sponsored numerous community activities, including entering a float into two holiday parades—a first for the organization.

They are proud to report that hi was successful in completing the City of Hamilton lease audit and performance appraisal without any issues. Management understands the importance of communicating in an open and transparent manner in order to achieve their goals and are committed to continually keeping passengers, partners, stakeholders and the communities they serve informed.

The success of the airport is tied strongly to the strength of its people. Management says they are very fortunate to have such a dynamic team of professionals working to make Hamilton International Airport the airport of choice. They know that those who have used the facilities love flying from Hamilton International Airport and comment frequently on the warm and friendly staff they encounter when using hi.

The airport team also takes great pride in welcoming new customers to hi … and all are encouraged to experience "the hi life" soon.

"I am proud of the team at Hamilton International," Mr. Koroscil says. "It is a team of experienced, enthusiastic, dedicated and innovative people, all key elements to our continued growth and ability to handle challenges effectively.

Each and every day the primary focus of everyone at hi is the customer, the passenger, the visitor."

In 2006 and 2007, the airport continued to invest in ensuring hi provides a high level of reliability to its customers and partners. The installation of a category II instrument landing system maximizes hi's ability to increase accessibility during inclement weather conditions and reduced visibility. Additional improvements include the installation of a new precision approach path indicator system, and upgrades to the airfield electrical system.

Check-in was made easier for airport customers with the installation of six new check-in kiosks. The majority of customers are able to check-in in under 60 seconds, wait times at check-in counters are reduced, and existing check-in services are supplemented.

The outbound baggage room was also expanded in size, and a new hold baggage screening system was installed to ensure compliance with security regulations.

In late 2006, hi began the expansion of its international arrivals area. The expansion will double the current space to accommodate the growing transborder and international business and all its customers who enjoy flying from Hamilton International Airport.

In 2006, 527,133 passengers used the airport, and air cargo tonnage was 84,500. There were 41,878 takeoffs and landings. There were 3,600 jobs (direct and indirect) associated with the airport, and $120-million in employment income, as well as $410-million in economic output.

In the future, it is estimated there will be a job base of 21,000, with $800-million in employment income and $2.5-billion in economic output. That's growth, that's progress.

Additionally, the Hamilton International Airport is also the country's largest inter-modal freighter airport and offers runway services that can accommodate fully-loaded wide-body international aircraft.

Airport operator TradePort International Corporation, through its operating subsidiary Hamilton International Airport Limited, is responsible for the management, operation and development of the Hamilton International Airport.

During the 40-year lease term, all airport land remains the property of the City of Hamilton and TradePort pays property taxes and rent to the city. Upon lease expiry in March 2036 all infrastructure and facilities developed by TradePort and its tenants at the airport become property of the City of Hamilton.

TradePort International Corporation is majority owned by YVR Airport Services (Hamilton) Ltd., a subsidiary of the Vancouver International Airport Services which operates 18 airports in 7 countries, including The Bahamas, Canada, Chile, Cyprus, Dominican Republic, Jamaica and the Turks and Caicos Islands.

TradePort is a consortium of Westpark Developments, a local Hamilton land development company, the Labourers International Union of North America (LIUNA) and YVR Airport Services.

Vancouver Airport Services (YVRAS) is the sole owner of Tradeport. YVRAS is North America's leading global airport investment, management and development company with 18 airports in seven countries that process almost 27 million passengers annually. Since 1995, YVRAS has successfully managed 19 seamless airport transitions from public to private management. Every airport is unique and global experience is used to bring world-class operating standards and commercial success to airports in vastly different competitive and cultural environments.

Said Frank O'Neill, President of YVRAS at the time: "We're excited to grow our involvement in Canada's second busiest airport and to play a significant role in taking

19

Hamilton International airport to the next level. By building on our past successes, we will work to ensure that the airport continues to be an important part of the community of Hamilton and the Ontario and Canadian economies."

The Board of Directors of TradePort International Corporation provides governance for the airport. The board is comprised of five qualified and eligible members that are elected or re-elected on an annual basis. The board must consist of at least one and a maximum of nine members at any time. The board may from time to time appoint one or more committees or advisory bodies as it may deem advisable.

Management seeks to achieve Hamilton International Airport's full potential by being one of Canada's five busiest passenger airports, and the number one air freighter gateway in Canada.

Mr. Koroscil proudly highlights the airport's progress in the past year alone.

"On the commercial side of things, May 2007 saw the arrival of flyglobespan," he said. "They offer daily flights from the convenience of Hamilton International to London-Stansted, London-Gatwick, Manchester, Glasgow, Dublin, Shannon Airport, Belfast, Edinburgh, Newcastle, Exeter, Birmingham, Doncaster and Liverpool. flyglobespan's decision to provide service from Hamilton was significant as this is the first time in the history of the airport to have an international air carrier.

"flyglobespan, collectively with WestJet, Air Canada and our tour operators Sunquest and Transat, ensures that Hamilton International offers more Canadian, UK, and sun destinations than ever before with excellent global connectivity.

"Passengers, guests and visitors to Hamilton International can enjoy the benefits of self service check-in kiosks, a duty free shop, foreign exchange kiosk, an expanded domestic arrivals area, wireless internet, on-demand limo service, a tourism information centre, a Kidz Korner activity area. retail, food and beverage concessions, including two Tim Horton's operations. We have also expanded our international arrivals area, offer improved lounge seating and airbus service between London, Ontario and Hamilton.

"Without a doubt, Hamilton International possesses the air-side and terminal capacity to service a considerable increase in passenger and cargo traffic and can contribute significantly to the passenger and cargo needs of both the Greater Golden Horseshoe and regional economies."

Hamilton International is also noted as being the largest dedicated inter-modal freighter airport in the country and services all major Canadian and International destinations. hi cargo partners include Cargojet, BAX Global, DHL, UPS and Purolator. The airport's distinct geographic position makes hi a cargo gateway to the North American market

The competitive advantage airport is uniquely positioned to be a premier cargo gateway to the North American market. It provides an ideal location for cargo carriers from Europe, Asia and South America, looking to transport their goods into North America.

The airport is strategically located to service its immediate catchment area as well as the northeastern and central United States – the largest market in North America. The airport is at the centre of it all. Some of the key points to remember include:

1) Strategic location along two NAFTA super-corridors;
2) 24 hour, 7-day a week operations including 24-hour Canada Customs;
3) No peak period charges;
4) No air congestion and no ground delays leading to rapid turnaround of aircraft;
5) Plentiful dedicated apron space;
6) Operational flexibility on the aprons with airside, truck to

air, air to truck transfers;

7) Nearby highway network provides one-day truck access to 150 million consumers;

8) North America's largest courier companies are located there;

9) Cargo business development is Hamilton's number one priority;

10) Ongoing airport infrastructure projects and improvements;

11) 10,000-foot runway capable of handling any size aircraft;

12) And a multi-tenant cargo facility.

The airport is the first stop on the polar route. Cargo carriers can service a wide area stretching from New York to Detroit and Chicago with one flight, one stop.

The airport is connected to the major North American and regional trade corridors. An excellent highway network provides easy access to Ontario, Quebec, and the U.S. In addition, hi is connected to excellent rail and water links for all forms of intermodal transportation.

The rapidly-changing global economy demands the most efficient transportation and distribution system. Key success factors for air-cargo distribution include: a large catchment area; a central and strategic location; multi-modal capability and competitive pricing.

Centred within one of the largest population centres in North America, the airport has a total catchment area of of 3.25-million customers, and its two-hour catchment is about 9-million customers.

The airport enjoys a strategic geographic location. North America's North-East Super Region is the world's greatest economic powerhouse. Hamilton International airport is centrally located in the centre of this Super Region, and alongside the NAFTA Super-Corridor – a series of super-highways that deliver raw materials, parts and inventory, and finished goods between plants in Canada, the United States and Mexico. In 2002, over 57 million metric tonnes, representing over $223-billion of raw materials and finished goods passed along highways adjacent to the Hamilton International Airport on the way to market. The reason for this is simple, hi has a one-day truck catchment of over 150 million consumers – a larger truck catchment than New York, Montreal, Toronto, or Detroit.

The Hamilton International Airport is strategically located for global markets, as well. Situated directly along the polar trade routes connecting the North-East Super Region to emerging markets in Asia and Eastern Europe, hi is the most economical airport for air cargo shipments between these markets.

The Hamilton International Airport enjoys close connectivity with highway, rail, and marine transportation. It has direct linkage to Ontario's 400 series of super-highways. These connect directly to the U.S. highway network.

The main trunk line of Canadian National Railways (www.cn.ca) is nearby the Hamilton airport.

The Port of Hamilton (www.hamiltonport.ca) is considered the finest natural harbour on the Great Lakes. It is located at the western end of Lake Ontario - strategically positioned for access to Canada's industrial heartland and major markets in the United States. Twelve million tonnes of cargo and nearly 700 ships move through the harbour in an average year. Whether you ship steel, fertilizer, grain, or automobiles, the Port of Hamilton can handle your cargo.
Landing and handling fees at Hamilton are one of the airport's biggest competitive advantages.

Hamilton International Airport is Canada's largest integrated courier airport. Home to major operations of UPS Canada Ltd, Purolator, and CargoJet. Hamilton's air cargo success is due to its 24-7 operational capability and strategic geographic location.

UPS (United Parcel Service) is the world's largest express carrier and has a 47,800-square-foot sort centre at the Hamilton International Airport, the international hub of its Canadian operations.

Purolator Courier, which operates Canada's largest dedicated air express fleet, has a 93,359-square-foot sorting facility at hi. The Hamilton International Airport is the hub of its Canadian route network.

Cargojet Canada Ltd. provides a premium overnight air cargo service into 12 major city centres throughout Canada.

The Hamilton International Airport has a number of freight forwarders and custom brokers providing timely customs clearance, surface transportation, "global" ocean and air freight forwarding services.

They are: Federated Custom Brokers (www. federated-group.com); Livingston International (www. livingstonintl.com); UPS Supply Chain Solutions (www. ups-scs.ca); WestJet Cargo (www.westjet.com); Cargojet Airways Ltd. (www.cargojet.com); and Ontario Flightcraft (www.flightcraft.ca).

As well, Hamilton is the preferred Toronto-area airport for many North American and international charter cargo airlines including: Amerijet International, Ameristar Jet Charter, Cargojet Airways, Castle Aviation, Contract Air Cargo, Custom Air Transport, First Air/Air NWT, Flair Airlines, Florida West Air, Kelowna Flightcraft, Kitty Hawk Airways, Knighthawk Air Express, Murray Aviation, Polet, and USA Jet.

The following companies and services call the Hamilton International Airport home: Air Canada Ground Handling Services, Flagship International Aviation, Esso Aviation, Glanford Aviation Services Ltd., Jetport, Ontario Flightcraft, Kelowna Flightcraft, Peninsulair, Swissport Canada Handling Inc., The Canadian Warplane Heritage

Museum, and The Royal Canadian Air Force Association. Airport management was pleased to compile an impressive list of highlights from 2006:

1) WestJet Airlines enhanced its schedule, offering Orlando as a new destination and Vancouver as a direct flight from hi. WestJet also increased its summer flying
from hi more than 50 per cent over 2005;

2) Air Canada Jazz celebrated a successful first year with daily service to Ottawa and Montreal;

3) Sunquest/Skyservice Airlines returned to hi providing direct service to popular sun destinations Cancun and Punta Cana;

4) Transat Holidays continued to offer service to Cancun, Punta Cana and Puerto Plata;

5) Aeromexico had 18 Mexican tourist charter flights from hi in 2006;

6) The airport announced the May 2007 start-up for flyglobespan with daily flights to 13 UK
and Irish destinations;

7) Cargojet Airways, with hi as its hub, increased its flying by 30 per cent;

8) BAX Global, a transportation and logistics service provider, selected Cargojet as its operator to serve Southwestern Ontario, Montreal and the BAX Global Inc. hub in Toledo, Ohio, via Hamilton International Airport;

9) Destination hi, the third annual event was designed for the travel trade industry and welcomed over 200 travel agents, hi supporters and partners;

10) The airport celebrated 10 years under the management of TradePort International;

11) A 45-foot flatbed was transformed into a spectacular 'hi float' showcasing Hamilton International Airport and its partners. In 2006, the 'hi float' participated in the 18th Annual Hamilton Santa Claus Parade and the 2nd Annual Stoney Creek Santa Claus Parade.

There were more destinations, air carrier partnerships and services than ever before.

John Dolbec, chief executive officer of the Hamilton Chamber of Commerce, is a frequent patron of the Hamilton Airport, both for business and leisure purposes, using the facilities up to five times a year.

"Hi is simply the best," he said.

Mr. Dolbec reiterated most of the earlier points made by Mr. Foxcroft, Mr. Koroscil and Mr. McMillan, but he had other insights, as well.

"If I have any choice in the matter, I will always choose flying Hamilton over Pearson and the reasons are simple [besides all the logistical points made by others]," he said. "Moreover, all of the flights that I have had out of Hamilton are using airlines that cost a fraction of what I would apply for airlines flying out of Pearson.

"Plus, staff seems to be much friendlier, more personable, and genuinely interested in us as people – not 'cattle' being herded through the system. In short, it is a much more 'civilized' experience.

"With many airlines and flights now flying out of Hamilton, it is possible with connecting flights to go virtually anywhere that you would want to travel out of Hamilton. The advantages of flying out of Hamilton are significant enough that it is even worth enduring the possible nuisance of connecting flights just to fly from Hamilton."

His most recent experiences are certainly reflective of his position.

"You can go virtually anywhere you can think of now, from Hamilton," he explained. "For example, just this June, via flyglobespan, my wife and I flew to Budapest, very conveniently and at about half the cost of what it have been via Pearson.

"Then, the next week, I took a quick flight from Hamilton to Ottawa via [Air Canada] Jazz to join my son at the family cottage in Quebec. "The next weekend, I flew Westjet to Edmonton out of Hamilton for a quick two-day trip. All inexpensive and convenient – it's almost just like when I used to hop on a bus when I was younger - it's really not like flying at all."

So, we can see that Hamilton International Airport is an entrepreneurial, action-oriented airport management company. They do this by providing customers and community a convenient, hassle-free high-value airport experience which maximizes stakeholder value.

They have strategic objectives, such as expanding passenger air service, increasing air cargo traffic, enhancing revenue opportunities, promoting regional tourism and strategic investment in infrastructure and facilities.

Hamilton International Airport is the low-cost, convenient alternative that is helping to redefine travel options and opportunities in the region through its fresh customer-service model, effective, collaborative partnerships, growth-oriented investment and track-record for success.

In all decisions and daily activities, Hamilton International Airport incorporates the "hi 5 values" when dealing with customers, partners, co-workers, corporate resources and the environment.

In their words, that means take action, be responsive, take initiative and find timely solutions, be innovative, think creatively, be resourceful, maintain flexibility, act safe, understand risk follow procedures and use common sense, show respect, be understanding, show compassion and act with integrity.

Or, as Mr. Dolbec puts it: "With the dramatic increase in flights and airlines using Hamilton over the past few years, it is an absolutely great, convenient, inexpensive, personable and comfortable way to fly.

"Just try to tell me why would you want to fly from anywhere else?"

27

2

There is no better starting point to find out about the history of the Hamilton Airport than the Canadian Warplane Heritage Museum, located right on airport property.

And, if you really want to get the inside scoop on the early years, you can find no better source than one Bill Tourtel, age 81, who's been around the Hamilton aviation scene since the 1940s. Bill loves to talk and that serves him well, since he continues to be an airport fixture as a tour guide at the museum.

Bill, who was in the Canadian air force during World War II, actually learned to fly in one of the first Canadian airports, Hamilton Municipal Airport, which he called "East End Airport" off Barton Street in Hamilton.

"I learned in a J3 Cub," he said. "I had my licence in 15 hours; nowadays it takes about 60 or 70 hours. But of course there's a lot more to do.

"The government even paid for some of it; they wanted pilots."

When the "East End Airport" shut down around 1956, Bill moved on to the Hamilton Airport, which was more or less served as a reserve air force airport up until that time.

He ended up operating as a bush pilot, as well as

being the chief flying instructor for Peninsular Air Services Ltd. (now known as PeninsularAir, a current airport tenant). Times were different then, and employees did more than fly airplanes. Bill recalls towing a lawnmower behind a pickup truck to cut the long grass growing through cracks in the runway.

"I even helped paint numbers on the runway," he laughs. Bill's experiences are only one of many, however, as Hamilton and area residents have been interested in aviation since 1911.

The first airport in the Hamilton area, privately-owned and named Elliot Field on Beach Road, was opened in 1926. Designated as an "air harbour," it housed the Hamilton Aero Club and a flight school. One of its first graduates was Eileen Vollick, Canada's first female pilot.

The second local airport, called the Hamilton Municipal Airport, was opened by the City of Hamilton near Red Hill Creek. It featured two hard surface runways with several commercial operations and by 1931 was equipped for night flying.

A civil aviation report from that year stated: "Hamilton Airport is owned by the City which has spent $300,000 on its development without assistance from the government. With the exception of Vancouver, no city has made a larger investment in aviation."

Hamilton Municipal Airport remained in operation until a final transition at the military airfield at Mount Hope took place in the 1950s, allowing for public use.

Hamilton's airport at Mount Hope was built on its present site in October 1940, as a wartime air force training station..

The genesis of Hamilton Airport typifies the facilities constructed across Canada early in World War II to meet the needs of the British Commonwealth air-training plan. The airport was originally designed as a multi-purpose

29

military field and was used for flight training, air navigation, telegraphy and air gunnery. After World War II, an R.C.A.F. auxiliary squadron remained, and in 1946 the Hamilton Aero club took occupancy of several vacated buildings and obtained a license for the airfield in 1947.

Between 1945 and 1963, a gradual uncoordinated transition from military establishment to a public facility occurred. Responsibility for the operation and maintenance of the facility involved federal, local and private organizations.

In 1952, the City of Hamilton applied for the licence and by the mid 1950s about one-third of aircraft movements were military (including light cargo) while the remainder were predominantly local general aviation. In 1961, Nordair established a scheduled "seaway route" using Dart Heralds and DC-3's but abandoned it in1962 due to lack of traffic.

In 1963, Department of National Defence declared the Hamilton Airport at Mount Hope surplus to its needs and the Department of Transportation assumed ownership and control.

In 1967, an agreement was reached whereby the City of Hamilton would assume responsibility for the maintenance and operation of the airport, and the D.O.T. would provide, maintain and operate a D.O.T. control tower and navigational aids.

From 1967 to 1996, Transport Canada supported the air operation through direct subsidy to cover operating deficits and by upgrading infrastructure to ensure the airport met acceptable operation standards.

In 1968, Nordair established a commercial air service at Hamilton and obtained authority for a Hamilton/Montreal and Hamilton/Pittsburgh service, which was inaugurated in May 1969.

In 1972, the federal government announced plans to upgrade existing airport facilities in Southwestern

Ontario and to continue studies to determine the long-term requirements of the area as a whole.

A review of passenger demand estimates indicated that an unexpected increase over previous forecasts would necessitate a complete upgrading of the passenger handling facilities.

Strong public opposition emerged over concern for the potentially disruptive social and environmental impacts associated with the construction of a new runway.

The Minister of Transportation at the time directed that a study be undertaken to determine the best location for the provision of facilities to service the needs of the Hamilton-Niagara area. The study began in early 1975. Two committees, the Citizens Ad Hoc Advisory Committee and the Intergovernmental Technical Co-ordinating Committee, were established to ensure relevant public input and co-ordination with various governments, federal departments, and agencies.

In the initial phase of the study, four concepts were identified for the development of the existing site and five alternative sites for a new airport for the Hamilton area were researched using the following criteria:
1) Engineering/technical factors;
2) Air traffic services;
3) Telecommunications;
4) Airspace;
5) Civil engineering;
6) Social/economic considerations;
7) Environmental impact;
8) Ecology and air quality;
9) Noise/displacement impact;
10) Agricultural impact;
11) Ground access considerations;
12) Regional planning considerations;
13) And costs.

Subsequent reports by the Ad Hoc Advisory Committee, and Transport Canada (with the Intergovernmental Committee's election to provide technical recommendations to Transport Canada) leaned in favour of improvements to the existing site.

In July of 1980, the expansion program to be undertaken was announced. This planned expansion was to consist of:

1) Construction of a new 2,400-metre by 60-metre (8,000-foot by 200-foot) east-west runway;
2) New and improved taxiways;
3) An expanded passenger aircraft apron;
4) New car parking facilities;
5) New passenger access roadway to the terminal;
6) Expanded air terminal building;
7) A new fire hall and emergency equipment;
8) And electrical, water and sewage services.

In order to begin construction of the new runway, additional property was purchased by the Crown. This involved the expropriation of various properties on Glancaster Road, Southcote Road and on Highway 6. Construction of the project began in the fall of 1981 and was completed in the early part of 1986.

Construction began with the expansion of the passenger aircraft apron and the remaining projects were staggered throughout the term. The runway configuration previous to the expansion consisted of three runways in a triangular pattern common to military air bases during wartime.

The groundside, designed in a rectangular grid, was comprised of a network of military barracks, administration buildings, workshops, and hangars, some of which are still functional and are being used for airport related purposes.

One of these runways was lengthened to 6,000 feet

and and equipped with a Non-CAT ILS system and low-intensity approach lights. This was the main runway until the completion of the expansion project.

The addition of the new east-west 8,000-foot runway, complete with the improved visual and electronic navigational aids, enhanced Hamilton airport's ability to attract larger aircraft. The new Air Terminal Building, completed in late 1985, was triple the size of the previous one, enabling HIA to process an estimated 450,000 passengers per year.

In October 1985, the operations and maintenance of the airport was transferred to the Regional Municipality of Hamilton-Wentworth from the City of Hamilton.

On February 15, 1993, a devastating fire destroyed Hangar Number 3, one of the Canadian Warplane Heritage hangars.

But on September 20, 1994, due to the importance and significance of the heritage museum in the community, Regional Council approved the construction of a new $12-million Canadian Warplane Heritage Museum with the assistance of Canada/Ontario Infrastructure Works Program funding. The federal and provincial governments contributed $4-million each to the project, the museum contributed $3-million, with another $1-million coming from the Region.

A sod-turning ceremony took place on September 24, 1994 and the Canadian Warplane Hertitage Museum opened its doors to the public on March 2, 1996.

From that point on, however, we see the airport taking a gradual path to public/private partnership.

In 1991 the annual report of the auditor general raised the issue of federal Transportation Department spending on airports. From 1992-1993, Transport Canada studied the feasibility of privatizing the airport system.

Then, in 1994, Transport Canada announced its National Airport Policy, designed in part to transfer airports to local authorities. In 1993, the Regional Municipality of Hamilton-Wentworth commissioned a study into the financial viability of Hamilton's airport. This study forecast future profits but also identified up to $60-million in capital spending required to bring the airport up to competitive levels.

In July 1995, the Region signed an agreement to enter into formal negotiations with Transport Canada to transfer ownership of the airport. At the same time, the Region began looking for private sector involvement in the management, marketing and development of the airport.

Led by local businessman and builder, Tony Battaglia, of WestPark Developments, and with the operational expertise of the Vancouver Airport Authority, TradePort International Corporation, in a competitive bidding process, was selected by the City of Hamilton to manage and operate the Hamilton International Airport. Also investing in the TradePort vision was the Hamilton local of the Labourers' International Union of North America (Liuna).

The Hamilton International Airport public/private partnership is based upon the lease-develop-operate model; the preponderance of risk is allocated to the private sector partner, TradePort International, which is responsible for all marketing, operating, and capital costs of the airport.

Prior to the partnership, the airport was running at a loss of almost $1-million annually. It now generates a profit, at no cost to taxpayers and a profit-sharing relationship with the City of Hamilton will soon take effect.

Since privatization, the airport-related workforce has grown from 726 to more than 1,300 full-time equivalent employees.

Under TradePort management, passenger traffic at the Hamilton terminal had increased from 90,000 in 1996 to approximately 900,000 by 2002, and continued to grow over the next five years. Air cargo increased by 50 per cent since

1996; and 91,000 metric tonnes of cargo passed through the airport in 2002.

Vancouver Airport Services (YVRAS) is the sole owner of TradePort International Corporation, which holds a 40-year lease with the City of Hamilton to develop, manage and operate the Hamilton International Airport.

YVRAS is North America's leading global airport investment, management and development company with 18 airports in seven countries that process almost 27 million passengers annually.

Since 1995, YVRAS has successfully managed 19 seamless airport transitions from public to private management. Every airport is unique and global experience is used to bring world-class operating standards and commercial success to airports in vastly different competitive and cultural environments.

"We have a strong vision for our network and that vision involves Hamilton," said George Casey, President and CEO of YVR Airport Services (YVRAS), "YVRAS has invested more money in Hamilton than in any other city where we operate. We are committed to growing Hamilton International Airport and we have a proven 10-year track record here. YVRAS is truly looking forward to building upon our current successes with hi."

For Ron Foxcroft, TradePort chairman and founder of Fox 40 International and chairman and CEO of Fluke Transportation Group Ltd., the privatization of the airport heralded a key turning point in its destiny.

"This is one of the best public/private partnerships in the entire area," he says. "It is a classic case of an entrepreneur [Tony Battaglia] having a vision for the airport and selling it to Liuna, who processed the first cheque in the TradePort history."

Mr. Foxcroft is known as a community ambassador for the city of Hamilton and was named Hamilton's

Distinguished Citizen of the Year in 1997.

He was awarded an Honourary Doctor of Laws degree from McMaster University in 2001 and named by Profit Magazine as one of the Top 10 Entrepreneurs of the Decade. His list of accomplishments is distinguished, but it is his invention of the Fox 40 Pealess whistle that has won him international acclaim. He is a highly sought after keynote presenter and travels the globe with his motivational Hamilton success story.

"TradePort was formed and they involved YVR," he recalls. "The result was an entrepreneur's vision coupled with expertise in airport operations.

"Immediately the City of Hamilton realized how wise it was for Hamilton to get out of the airport business. Immediately, the public and potential investors and customers started to get confidence in Hamilton Airport.

"Then in 2003 Tony Battaglia decided to turn the day-to-day over to airport people and Richard Koroscil was hired. Then in 2006, YVR bought 100 per cent ownership in TradePort. They have the greatest investment in Hamilton; more than any other of the 20-plus airports that they own or manage."

For Bill Tourtel, sitting in expansive, glassed-in meeting room above the museum, looking out at the modern operation, it's a long way from the days when he operated a snow plow to clear the outdated runways for Peninsula Air Services Ltd.

"It's a lot of fun meeting people and seeing how the planes and the airport has developed," he said, noting that the Hamilton Airport is Canada's largest dedicated courier/cargo airport and one of Canada's largest passenger airports.

But he points out there is no better place to start a trip down memory lane than a tour through the museum.

Canadian Warplane Heritage Museum is a living museum featuring the aircraft used by Canadians or Canada's military from the beginning of World War II up to the present. The museum's collection includes aircraft that really fly and several that remain on static display and are interactive workshops.

The museum strives to allow the visitor to experience and interact with the displays. One could climb into the cockpit of a real WWII trainer or a real jet fighter, or the Avro CF-100. The museum offers the visitor an educational experience that will take them back through Canadian history. You can see the display of WWII aircraft radios in the radio room and experience real-time operating radio station VA3CWM.

The museum also has interactive video displays, movies, photographs and memorabilia from Canadian history.

The museum is a non-profit organization whose mandate is to acquire, document, preserve and maintain a complete collection of aircraft that were flown by Canadians and the Canadian military services from the beginning of World War II to the present. Its role is to preserve the artifacts, books, periodicals and manuals relating to this mandate.

It's open year-round and has come a long way from relatively humble beginnings.

A collection of over 40 aircraft has grown through the friendship of Dennis J. Bradley and Alan Ness. Their love of aviation and their desire to maintain and preserve Canada's aviation history saw restoration projects that were not only great pieces of workmanship but airworthy examples.

Mr. Bradley and Mr. Ness approached friends Peter Matthews and John Weir to become partners with them to acquire the first aircraft, a Fairey Firefly. This aircraft was to become the masthead of the museum's advertising and stationery and continues to this day to be incorporated into logos, crests and memorabilia. A tribute to the four flying founders is located in the museum's main entrance.

In 1972, the group moved into part of a hangar at Hamilton Airport and started to seriously seek out other restoration projects or flying aircraft. A Harvard Mark IV was to be the next acquisition, followed over the years by Supermarine Spitfire, Corsair, Chipmunk and Tiger Moth.

Hangar 4, followed years later by Hangar 3 for restoration, was purchased and the aircraft collection and the volunteers finally had a home. The group applied for foundation status, to be governed by its own volunteers, operating as the Canadian Warplane Heritage. Meanwhile, sufficient interest was being shown by those watching the aircraft being restored. More enthusiasts wanted to become part of the growing activities and the membership program began.

The year 1975 saw the collection move into another area in Hangar 4 and the acquisition and restoration began on a B-25 Mitchell. The story of the arrival of this aircraft notes a strafing of the airfield and the bombing of the runway with watermelons. In the same year, the Westland Lysander and Cessna Crane joined the collection.

It is difficult to compress over 30 years of history into one short story. Many aircraft have joined the collection, or have been traded or sold. Tragedy struck in 1977 at the Canadian International Air Show. Alan Ness lost his life when the Fairey Firefly he was piloting crashed into Lake Ontario.

The aircraft was replaced and Ness' memory was commemorated by the awarding of the 'Alan Ness Memorial Trophy,' given annually to a deserving member of the museum.

The most ambitious restoration undertaking to date has been the Avro Lancaster. This aircraft stood guard over the Royal Canadian Legion Branch 109 in Goderich, Ontario. With the support of the Sulley Foundation, the Lancaster was acquired by Canadian Warplane Heritage in 1977.

There was a tremendous amount of work required to remove the 'Lanc' from its concrete pedestal and prepare it for transportation to Hamilton. The Canadian Forces accepted the transportation challenge, as a training mission to be performed by 450 Squadron. By moving the Lancaster to Hamilton via a Chinook helicopter airlift, valuable information was obtained by the military on the logistics of transporting large aircraft by helicopter. The aircraft arrived at the museum in 1979 and restoration began. It was not until 1988 that the CWH Lancaster Bomber, dedicated to Andrew Mynarski, VC, flew before 25,000 visitors.

In 1998, the museum celebrated the 10th anniversary of the first flight of the 'Lanc' with a gala dinner and dance, featuring the Spitfire Band, followed by other events throughout the year.

In 1978 the museum's first employee was hired. Today, full-time staff members work alongside volunteers in every aspect of the museum's day-to-day operations.

Membership in the Canadian Warplane Heritage Museum is open to all who share an interest in aircraft preservation. Funding for museum projects comes mainly from membership fees, private donations and sponsorships.

The provincial government, through the Ministry of Citizenship, Culture and Recreation, supports the museum through an operating grant. The federal government has recognized the importance of preserving certain aircraft of outstanding historical significance by certifying Canadian Warplane Heritage as a Cultural Property Institution.

On February 15, 1993, a large part of Hangar 3 was destroyed in a devastating fire. Included in the destruction of the hangar were five museum aircraft, the administrative offices, engineering records and all ground and maintenance equipment. The aircraft lost were the Hawker Hurricane, Grumman TBM Avenger, Auster, Stinson and Supermarine Spitfire. The fire spread quickly, reaching temperatures as high as 3,000 degrees Fahrenheit, through the north side of the building, requiring the assistance of four fire departments and 55 fire-fighters.

Volunteers who arrived to lend assistance could only watch helplessly as the fire was fought only a few feet away from the Avro Lancaster. At the time, the 'Lanc' was sitting on aircraft jacks. With fear that the roof might collapse, it was hours before the decision was made to allow the wheels to be installed and the aircraft removed. Also saved that day were two restoration projects, the Fleet Finch and Bristol Bolingbroke.

The museum battled back to design and build a 108,000 square-foot delta-wing-shaped building. With the support of the Canada-Ontario Infrastructure Works Program, all three levels of government supported a new site that would house all operations of the museum under one roof.

It was officially opened by the museum's patron, His Royal Highness the Prince of Wales, on April 26, 1996.

The museum now houses over 40 aircraft, and also an extensive aviation gift shop and exhibit gallery.

Special events take place throughout the year and facilities including the main aircraft exhibit area can be rented for private events.

You can book a group tour of the facility, and you might just meet up with Bill Tourtel.

"I don't fly anymore," Bill laughs, "but I haven't left aviation entirely."

The tours are available to groups of 20 persons or more with arrangements made in advance. Many of the groups that visit are school children, learning the theory of flight, aircraft design or military history.

The museum is living proof that Hamilton's role in Canadian aviation history is indisputable. And the tradition continues.

3

While gazing out onto a runway at Hamilton International Airport and seeing work crews rushing about on tow motors, loading cargo planes, it's easy to let one's mind drift back; back to the time when World War II broke out and Hamilton's aviation destiny changed forever.

Yes, Hamilton quickly mobilized to send troops, but it also played a key role in the British Commmonwealth air training plan, with a Royal Canadian Air Force training station opening at Mount Hope.

In a book written by Margaret Houghton, an archivist in the special collections department at the Hamilton Public Library, a vivid picture is painted about those early days; a picture much different than one sees today at the booming privatized airport.

Entitled Hamilton at War: On the home front, the book contains a short section that details how – even back then – the seeds of a civic airport were being sown.

It was 1940, and an announcement noted that negotiations for the purchase of 1,600 acres of land in the Mount Hope area were almost completed. The cost of the land was $80 an acre, for a grand total of $125,000. The land was to be developed as a "huge" airport to be developed for air force training.

In an excerpt from the book, the scene unfolded like this: "By August 1940 the buildings were going up and by

October of 1940 they were finishing the landing strips.

"On November 23, 1940 No. 10 Elementary Flying School was opened by Air Commodore G. E. Brookes, air officer commanding No. 1 training command of the R.C.A.F. Students were already at the school and learning to fly under the auspices of the Hamilton Flying Training School, limited.

"In June of 1941 No. 33 Air Navigation School, operated by officers of the Royal Air Force for the training of young English lads as observers opened next door to the Elementary Flying School. In command of the school was Wing Commander C.H. Brill sent from England where he had been second-in-command of a Royal Air Force station.

"Entering the school is like going to a little piece of England; on all sides you hear accents which those who know English dialects would be able to identify as native to various parts of the Old Country. The personnel, only recently arrived in Canada, are still trying to figure their money in terms of dollars and cents, still trying not to jump out of their seats when they hear a railway locomotive's bell. (In England, bells will sound only when the invader has come.)"

"Training at the school goes beyond the observers' training course originally laid down under the British Commonwealth Air Training Plan. In the old days, the observer in a British bomber, who makes the calculations which keep the machine on its course and guides it to its objective – possibly an arms factory deep in Germany – depended mainly on what is called dead-reckoning navigation.

"Dead reckoning navigation depends on the ability of the observer to check the course every now and then with known landmarks which are indicated on his map and to correct his course accordingly.

"But today, the bomber usually flies high above the

clouds, where it is not possible to see the ground at all, and most bombing flights are done at night when it isn't possible to see anything on the blacked-out countryside of Europe.

"So, at No. 33 Air Navigation school and at the other similar schools now in operation or being erected in different parts of Canada, observers-to-be are taught astral or celestial navigation.

"Some of the British 'lads' were so taken with the Hamilton area that they returned after the war, settling down with their Hamilton 'lassies' and raising families."

So as early as September 1940, the idea of the training facility evolving into a municipal civic airport after the war was being seriously considered. The decision was made easier since the other existing airport in the east end of Hamilton was landlocked and incapable of dealing with modern aircraft or expansion.

In November 1943, Hamilton Mayor William Morrison went to Ottawa to talk to the Honorable C.D. Howe, federal minister of munitions and supply, about the Mount Hope airport.

News bulletins of the day announced: "Dealing with reports emanating from Toronto that the government proposed to erect a large commercial airport north of the Queen City after the war, Mayor Morrison pointed out to Mr. Howe that such a port should be located between Toronto and Hamilton in order to serve the Hamilton and Niagara peninsula area. His Worship explained that Hamilton was a centre of great industrial and business activity, and the location of a commercial airport anywhere but on a site between Hamilton and Toronto would minimize the usefulness of the port."

Mr. Howe intimated that Hamilton would receive every consideration and, following the war, the Mount Hope airport would be turned over to the city for use as a civic facility, to operate and maintain.

At the end of the war, that is exactly what happened.

Mr. Tourtel recalls the years when the city of Hamilton and, later, the Regional Municipality of Hamilton, were in charge as a being much different than we see today with the privatized airport.

Upgrades to the airport were few and far between, he said, but the period was not lacking in colourful anecdotal recollections.

"There was considerable training going on during that period, with as many as three schools running," he said.

"Some commercial operators such as Nordair used to run a service to Ottawa and Montreal. But generally, there weren't a lot of improvements.

"There was one particularly dangerous moment, as I recall... There was not even a control tower at one time and it was just expected that pilots would broadcast their flight intentions on the local Unicom frequency.

"One of the runways had a hill on it, so much so that an aircraft at one end of the runway could not see another aircraft at the other end. One morning, at the same time, two aircraft chose to take off at opposite ends. Let's just say it became interesting when they approached each other at the middle.

"Some semblance of order came when a control tower was eventually installed."

"But those years of government-control were mostly a time when few people, generally, realized the potential of an airport near the city."

Enter John Carr Munro, who the airport is named after and who is now remembered as one of Hamilton's political giants.

Mr. Munro had always been a leader in efforts to expand and modernize Hamilton Harbour. By the 1970s, his hard work had turned Hamilton Harbour into one of Canada's major deep water ports, creating thousands of jobs, and producing millions of dollars in economic output.

Then he turned his attention to the airport. Expanding the Hamilton airport into a regional transportation hub had always been a dream of Hamilton politicians, but it took Mr. Munro to turn the dream into a reality.

By the early 1980s, Mr. Munro secured over $55-million in federal investment for what was then known as Mount Hope Airport.

The airport's first major expansion was announced in July, 1980, and it included the construction of a new 8,000 ft. east-west runway, new and improved taxiways, an expanded passenger aircraft apron, new car parking facilities, new passenger access roadway to the terminal, an expanded air terminal building, and other related airport services.

The new east-west 8,000-foot runway, 12L/30R, improved visual and electronic navigational aids, enabling the airport to accommodate larger aircraft. The Passenger Terminal Building, completed in late 1985, was triple the size of the previous one, allowing the airport to process up to 450,000 passengers per year at an acceptable level of service.

When a special ceremony was held Sunday, April 5, 1998, to celebrate the naming of the airport in his honour, Mr. Munro received many congratulatory salutations.

"Naming the airport after John Munro is an appropriate celebration of his sense of hope, potential, and his legacy," said Terry Cooke, former Hamilton-Wentworth regional chairman.

"Hamilton's airport has always been at the bottom of Transport Canada's priority list. That we're on the list at all is a tribute to John," said Jack MacDonald, former Hamilton mayor.

"John Munro has done a hell of a lot for Hamilton. He's put us on the map. He's one of the last of the good guys in the political world," trumpeted Angelo Mosca, former Hamilton Tiger Cats' player.

And, said Tony Battaglia, the original president
of TradePort International Corporation: "Mr. Munro is,
without question, worthy of public recognition for his long
and impressive record of public service ... bringing the
infrastructure of Hamilton International Airport to its current
fine condition."

Today, visitors to hi enjoy the results of over 60 years
of transition and change.

The airport is one of the easiest to navigate, with
ample and affordable parking, short walking distances and
quick exit times.

Once inside, visitors can reap the benefits of
improved concession and retail development. In 2007 alone,
five new food service and retail concepts were introduced
at the airport, including two Tim Horton's stores, On The
Fly retail, The Escarpment Lounge and Coyote Jack's Road
House.

"We've listened closely to the feedback received about
our services," said Mr. Koroscil. "In fact, a recent customer
satisfaction survey revealed that 95 per cent surveyed wanted
to see a Tim Horton's located in the Air Terminal Building
at hi. As a result, we have added two Tim Horton's locations
– one pre-Security and one post-Security."

Compass Group Canada, the world's largest
foodservice and facilities management company working
in more than 60 countries around the world, is the current
operator of concession services at hi and they have chosen
to grow with the airport. Local staffing will remain the
same, and fast, friendly service will continue to be offered
to complement the hi philosophy. The total area for the new
concession and retail is 1,940 square feet.

"Compass Group Canada is very excited about
this opportunity," said Eric Cameron, regional director
(Chartwells) Compass Group Canada. "We've renewed our
partnership and taken the concession and retail program at

Hamilton International to the next level. Our pricing will be competitive and the experience enjoyable."

There's also wireless internet connection throughout the terminal, and visitors can use their laptops or access two kiosks in the main concourse. There is an airport shuttle service, taxis and a limousine-on-demand service, as well as car rentals, making it an easy 20-minute trip from the airport to downtown Hamilton..

WestJet and Air Canada Jazz are its two main passenger carriers. A recent addition is Flyglobespan, which flies daily between London, Manchester and Glasgow, as well as other destinations in Great Britain.

There are frequent flights from British Columbia and the West, as well as from most points east, such as Ottawa, Montreal, Halifax, Moncton, St Johns and various international destinations.

A quick rundown of key airport commercial tenants shows the great strides hi has taken in the past few years:

WESTJET

WestJet was founded in 1996 by Clive Beddoe, Mark Hill, Tim Morgan and Donald Bell, four Calgary entrepreneurs who saw an opportunity to provide low-fare air travel across western Canada. The team researched other successful airlines in North America – in particular low-cost carriers. Following the primary examples of Southwest Airlines and Morris Air, they determined that a similar model could be successful in Western Canada.

They spent the subsequent months developing a comprehensive business plan and financial model. With this information in hand, a number of local business people were approached and within 30 days the needed capital was raised.

After purchasing the three original Boeing 737-200 aircraft, a second offering to retail and institutional investors was completed in January 1996, raising the necessary capital to begin operations.

On February 29, 1996, WestJet started flight operations with 220 employees and three aircraft to the cities of Vancouver, Kelowna, Calgary, Edmonton and Winnipeg. Later in 1996, WestJet added Victoria , Regina and Saskatoon to its western route network. In 1997, WestJet began service to Abbotsford/Fraser Valley, and in 1999 WestJet added Thunder Bay, Prince George and Grande Prairie to its service area.

But 1999 marked a major milestone for WestJet, completing its initial public offering of 2.5 million common shares in July of that year. It was an exciting day for all WestJetters, representing the achievement of a key business goal and raising the necessary capital for expansion of the company into the coming years. With the help of lead underwriters, CIBC World Markets, and the dedicated executive team, WestJet made a successful transition to a public company. The capital raised from the offering was used for the purchase of additional aircraft, as well as construction of a new head office and hangar facilities in Calgary.

Opportunity arose for WestJet in 1999 with the unprecedented change and restructuring of Canada's airline industry. In December 1999, WestJet announced that it would be extending its successful low-fare airline across Canada. Between March and June 2000, the company added service to the Eastern Canadian cities of Hamilton, Moncton and Ottawa.

It was at this time that Hamilton's airport became the eastern hub.

In 2000, WestJet's founders were honoured as 'The Ernst & Young Entrepreneur of the Year' for Canada, in recognition of the contributions they made to Canadian travellers and the lives of all of WestJet's people and shareholders. In 2001, WestJet added new service to Fort McMurray, Comox, and limited addition flights to Brandon.

In 2001, WestJet also added its first four Next-Generation Boeing 737-700 aircraft. Also, in 2001, the team of founders received an international entrepreneurship award for outstanding teamwork.

WestJet added service to two new Ontario destinations in 2002, in London and Toronto. In February of 2002, the corporation successfully offered three million common shares yielding net proceeds of $78.9-million. The proceeds would fund aircraft additions, spare parts and a third flight simulator. WestJet was also named one of Canada's top 100 employers that year.

Service to the new markets of Halifax, Windsor, Montréal, St. John's and Gander was also established in 2002.

WestJet's fleet of Next-Generation Boeing 737 aircraft, featuring new aircraft with leather seats and more leg room, began transborder service in the fall of 2004. The cities of Los Angeles, San Francisco, Phoenix, Fort Lauderdale, Tampa, Orlando and New York were added to the new U.S. route network. Service to Palm Springs, Maui, Honolulu and Fort Myers (seasonal) began in 2005.

Celebrating over 10 years in business, WestJet now employs over 6,000 people and has carried over 9.4-million guests. Its current 23 Canadian destinations include Hamilton, Victoria, Comox, Vancouver, Abbotsford/Fraser Valley, Prince George, Kelowna, Grande Prairie, Calgary, Edmonton, Fort McMurray, Saskatoon, Regina, Winnipeg, Thunder Bay, London, Toronto, Ottawa, Montréal, Moncton, Charlottetown, Halifax and St. John's. Its 10 current American destinations are Honolulu, Maui, Los Angeles, Palm Springs (seasonal), Las Vegas, Phoenix (seasonal), Tampa , Orlando, Fort Myers (seasonal) and Fort Lauderdale, West Palm Beach (seasonal). Internationally, WestJet flies seasonal service to Nassau, Bahamas .

JETPORT

Jetport was designed and built by a business traveler – Ron Joyce, the Hamilton multi-millionaire and co-founder of the Tim Horton's chain – for business travellers.

At Hamilton Airport, Jetport's large private ramp, spacious boardroom and comfortable pilots' quiet room help to make stays enjoyable and relaxing for clients. Constructed in 1997, it brought to hi what it previously lacked: a modern facility solely dedicated to servicing corporate and private aviation.

Its staff is pleased to arrange customs, hotels, rental cars, catering and even golf. Jetport's fully-heated 30,000-square-foot hangar can accommodate aircraft as large as a Global Express. Conveniently located off taxiway 'D', Jetport offers clients the largest private ramp and heated hangar on the field.

Because Jetport operates its own charter department, customers receive great service, a clean environment and a friendly and knowledgeable staff.

Jetport's experienced personnel will fly you to your destination in executive aircraft luxury. The modern charter fleet includes a range of aircraft from turbo-prop to wide-bodied jets with intercontinental range all equipped with state of the art navigation systems. Jetport can fly to major airports as well as thousands of smaller airports getting clients closer to their destination.

Jetport's   fleet includes a Challenger 604, a Gulfstream 100, a King Air 350, and a Cessna Caravan 208 on amphibious floats. Jetport also has a Eurocopter EC-155 helicopter with an eight-seat executive interior. And Jetport staff will arrange flights and can also assist with customs, hotels, rental cars and catering.

Says Todd DiPaolo, chief pilot for Jetport: "Due to our business model and management structure we've enabled positive growth, and a continued effort for future development. "Not only do we offer an economical savings advantage, but we are a logical alternative to the Toronto airport due to our geographical location; a super fit for business executives or celebrities who require anonymity."

FLYGLOBESPAN

Beginning in May, 2007, hi made a major step forward by offering flyglobespan services, with more than 10 destinations in the United Kingdom.

Flyglobespan is a wholly-owned subsidiary of The Globespan Group, a company established in 1974.
Said Mr. Koroscil at the time: "This is great news for hi. With London, England as our largest international market, travellers will be able to choose from 10 flights a week to two convenient airports."

One of Britain's fastest growing airlines, flyglobespan was voted airline of the year ear by the Scottish British Airlines Association in 2005.

"This reinforces flyglobespan's commitment to the Toronto, Hamilton and greater Southwestern Ontario markets," said Tom Dalrymple, flyglobespan chairman and managing director. "We're very excited about our partnership with Hamilton International Airport."
The airline had its first flight in April 2002. In 2007 it operated 14 Boeing 737 aircraft to a range of destinations within Europe.

Long-haul operations began in June of 2006 with a Boeing 767-300ER providing a daily service between Glasgow and Orlando in a three-service configuration. The addition of two further 767-300ERs and four 757-200ERs all-in-three service configuration will allow the airline to expand its operation even further into Canada, South Africa and the United States.

Flyglobespan believes its new and nearly-new aircraft offer many advantages, saying that its technology is up to the latest industry standards, and its fleet is equipped with the quietest and most economical engines. This enables flyglobespan, they say, to save operating costs and increase its competitiveness, as well as making an effective contribution to environmental protection.

AIR CANADA JAZZ

In January 2001, a newly-merged carrier called Air Canada Regional Inc. took to the skies. At that time a wholly-owned subsidiary of Air Canada, this company combined the individual strengths of our four regional airline brands – AirBC, Air Nova, Air Ontario, and Canadian Regional.

The challenging and complex process of consolidating these four companies was completed in 2002. The exciting achievement culminated with the launch of a new name and brand – Air Canada Jazz.

Air Canada Jazz is one of the largest regional airlines in the world, serving 84 destinations in Canada and the United States, and providing its customers with seamless connections to the worldwide networks of Air Canada and the Star Alliance.

With the most flights to the most communities in Canada, Air Canada Jazz considers itself an airline that brings together family, friends and business.

Headquartered in Halifax, Nova Scotia, Air Canada Jazz has regional offices and operational bases across Canada in Vancouver, Calgary, Toronto, London and Montreal.

When Air Canada took to the skies from hi in September, 2005, it heralded the fact that its passengers would see 55 per cent more destinations.

In June, 2005 Air Canada introduced new non-stop service between Hamilton-Ottawa and Hamilton-Montreal with connecting service to eastern Canadian destinations, including Deer Lake, Fredericton, Halifax, Quebec City, Moncton, St. John, New Brunswick, Charlottetown, St. John's Nfld., Bagotville, and Sydney, Nova Scotia, as well as European destinations of Paris, London, Munich and Frankfurt.

With the opportunity for same-day return trips, Air Canada Jazz operates daily non-stop frequencies between Hamilton and Montreal and Hamilton and Ottawa.

Hamilton International is very excited about having Air Canada Jazz at the airport. The daily non-stop frequencies between Hamilton and Ottawa, and Hamilton and Montreal certainly respond to the needs of the business traveller.

"Connecting service to European destinations opens doors to a tremendous untapped passenger volume potential," John Gibson, vice-president, marketing, at Hamilton International, said at the time.

ROYAL CANADIAN AIR FORCE ASSOCIATION

The 447 Wing of the Royal Canadian Air Force Association is a popular food and beverage establishment on the airport grounds, with many employees and local patrons.

PENINSULAIR

Peninsulair is hi's largest flight training facility. Many of the graduates are flying with major airlines throughout North America. Peninsulair operates a fleet of Piper aircraft including the Tomahawk, Cherokees, Warriors, Seminole and Navajo. Aircraft rentals are also available, as well as sightseeing flights and champagne flights over Niagara Falls

The company has a complete line of pilot supplies as well as aviation novelty items for sale. Their charters supply both cargo to corporate passenger service.

Available 24 hours a day, seven days a week, Peninsulair caters to small private aircraft as well as corporate jets. They provide ground handling for major airlines, as well as fuel, and aircraft maintenance.

COURIER SERVICES

Cargojet Canada Ltd.
Cargojet Airways, through its alliance partners and its subsidiary, Cargojet Canada Ltd., operates a network of nine B727-200AF in Canada, providing a premium overnight air cargo service into 12 major city centres throughout Canada, handling over 400,000 pounds of cargo each business night. Its headquarters are in Mississauga, Ontario, and the company currently employs over 400 people.

United Parcel Service
Hamilton Airport serves as the Canadian hub for UPS .
UPS Canada Ltd. has scheduled nightly flight operations at Hamilton. These aircraft consist of one B-757 and two B-

727s, with flights between the U.S. and Canada. UPS has invested in a $15-million sort centre, integrating its cross-Canada and U.S. transborder air cargo shipping. Domestic services within Canada are performed by All Canada Express, which operates two flights nightly, both are cargo B-727.

Purolator Courier

Purolator, Canada's largest air courier operator, has built its major cross-Canada sort centre in Hamilton. Purolator operates four to five nightly flights, all B-727 200s. These aircraft are flown domestically within Canada and operated by Ontario Flightcraft and Kelowna Flightcraft respectively.

FREIGHT FORWARDERS AND CUSTOM BROKERS

The Hamilton airport has a number of freight forwarders and custom brokers – including Federated Custom Brokers, Livingston International and UPS Supply Chain Solutions – providing timely customs clearance, surface transportation, and global ocean and air freight services.

All in all, an impressive, progressive operation at Hamilton Airport; a far cry from the humble beginnings that Bill Tourtel recalls with nostalgic fervour.

"When there was a lot of training going on at the airport, one of the commercial operators that basically ran the airport even cut the grass and plowed the snow," he said. "I remember one attempt to speed up cutting the weeds in the runway cracks was to pull a lawnmower behind a pickup truck!"

How times have changed. John C. Munro International Airport has certainly moved onward and upward.

4

With key components now in place at the Hamilton Airport, the future has never looked brighter.

The airport has been rapidly evolving since TradePort took over management about 10 years ago, and there is no indication that the steady progress will slow down any time soon.

In a recent study conducted for the airport by Hendershot Research Consultants of Hamilton, Mr. Koroscil was keen to report that findings showed there was a majority consensus that hi is a "key economic driver' for Hamilton.

Of the 600 participants randomly surveyed by phone across Hamilton, 92.5 per cent agreed to the statement that Hamilton airport is a key economic driver for Hamilton.

The findings showed that there is little doubt that the community recognizes the significance of the airport with respect to the city's financial development.

When asked about a change of opinion regarding the airport, 17.7% reported a change in their opinion of the airport over the past year, with the majority of this sample (72.6%) having experienced a positive change.

The most popular reasons for this positive change include: improvements, expansion and update of the parking lot, improvements to drop-off and pick-up areas, updates and expansions to waiting areas.

The survey also includes participants' responses regarding findings on the ownership of hi, usage of the airport, awareness of destinations and much more.

The study showed that there were currently 3,600 jobs (direct and indirect) tied into the airport, with a projection of growth potential to 21,000.

Employment income was $120-million with a hike to $800-million forecast. Economic output was marked at $410-million with potential for growth targeted at $2.5-billion.

Not figures to be scoffed at.

Additional announcements included:

There were more carrier partners, including Flyglobespan, WestJet Airlines, Air Canada Jazz, Mexicana, Aeromexico, Skyservice Airlines and Zoom;

Hi was the busiest multi-modal freighter airport in Canada, with cargo airlines UPS, Purolator, CargoJet, USA Jet and Bax Global onsite;

A significant increase in passenger traffic.

As part of its partnership with TradePort, which maintains a 40-year lease to develop, operate and maintain the airport, hi showed that the city of Hamilton maintains ownership of airport lands.

TradePort will subsidize any operating deficits, fund capital improvements, manage regulatory requirements, environmental and operating liabilities, and work with the city to "use best efforts' to maximize airport revenue.

The city, in turn, receives rent and property taxes (deferred at the beginning of the lease.)

"We invested in the public awareness study to find out how we can improve our services, and continue to be a key economic driver for this city," Mr. Koroscil said.

To that end, a number of interesting and telling results were documented.

Ownership of the airport:

An overwhelming 45% said they did not know who owned the airport, while 32% believed the city was the owner, and 11.8% named TradePort. A small percentage named the provincial or federal government, or 'other'.

Opinion of the airport:

All respondents were asked to indicate in their own words their personal opinion of Hamilton International.

The most frequently mentioned comments were: "I love it / great for city" (27.3%), followed by "nice / okay / good" (24.5%) and "convenient" (20.5%).

Respondents in Mount Hope (34%) and Ancaster (32%) were more likely to indicate "convenient" than among Hamilton respondents. (20.5%).

Of the negative comments, the most frequently mentioned was "would like more flights" (12.8%).

Based on the 600 respondents, only 4.3% overall mentioned that the airport was noisy. Respondents in Mount Hope (15.0%) and Ancaster (8.0%) were more likely to mention that the airport was noisy in comparison to Hamilton (.8%)

When asked, 17.7% reported a change in their opinion of the airport over the past year, with the majority of this sample (72.6%) having experienced a positive change. Of this sample, 18% of Hamilton respondents indicated that their opinion of Hamilton International had changed in the past year.

In comparison, only 11% of Mount Hope respondents indicated their opinion had changed, however, 23% of Ancaster respondents indicated their opinion had changed.

The most popular reasons for this positive change include: improvements, expansion and update of the parking lot. The survey also scored high on a favourability rating, with nearly 80% giving a positive opinion.

Key initiatives proposed by hi included continued expansion of flight alternatives – both passenger and cargo – and maintaining a close relationship with the city and community in Hamilton.

Mr. Koroscil was asked to again highlight the strides being taken, in the ongoing improvement and modernization of the airport.

As he noted: "On the commercial side of things, May 2007 saw the arrival of flyglobespan. They offer daily flights from the convenience of Hamilton International to London-Stansted, London-Gatwick, Manchester, Glasgow, Dublin, Shannon Airport, Belfast, Edinburgh, Newcastle, Exeter, Birmingham, Doncaster and Liverpool. Flyglobespan's decision to provide service from Hamilton was significant as this is the first time in the history of the airport to have an international air carrier.

"Flyglobespan, collectively with WestJet, Air Canada and our tour operators Sunquest and Transat , Hamilton International offers more Candian, UK, and sun destinations than ever before with excellent global connectivity.

"Passengers, guests and visitors to Hamilton International can enjoy the benefits of self service check-in kiosks, a duty free shop, foreign exchange kiosk, an expanded domestic arrivals area, wireless internet, on-demand limo service, a tourism information centre, a Kidz Korner activity area. retail, food and beverage concessions, including two Tim Horton's concessions.

"We have also expanded our international arrivals area, offer improved lounge seating and airbus service between London, Ontario and Hamilton.

"Without a doubt, Hamilton International possesses the airside and terminal capacity to service a considerable increase in passenger and cargo traffic and can contribute significantly to the passenger and cargo needs of the Greater Golden Horseshoe as well as the regional economy.

"Hamilton International is also noted as being the largest dedicated inter-modal freighter airport in the country and services all major Canadian and international destinations. hi cargo partners include Cargojet, BAX Global, DHL, UPS and Purolator. The airport's distinct geographic position makes hi a cargo gateway to the North American market."

Encapsulated, the successes of the airport drive home just how far removed the operation is from its pre-privatization days.

Ron Foxcroft, TradePort chairman, adamantly believes that the airport is providing a substantial boost Hamilton's profile. "It is helping the image of Hamilton," he said. "Hamilton's image is suffering, and the fact is: that the airport is doing so many good things.

"The impression that Hamilton is not friendly to business is being improved. Hamilton must attract business. In its heyday when Hamilton was known as The Ambitious City, the assessment was approximately 70% business and 30% residential. Very healthy. Today the assessment is approximately the opposite, which is very unhealthy.

"To be vibrant, you must show people that Hamilton is friendly to business and you must have a vibrant airport, transportation and harbour. We are developing all three. It must move quickly as the city is predicting zero increase in 2008 in assessment. You need business to be a healthy city, and business creates jobs.

"The airport is important to satisfying these needs."

Like others, Mr. Foxcroft believes that the airport is the economic engine that is going to make a key impact on the revitalization of the Hamilton image and economy.

"I wish every person in Hamilton could see how skilled the management of YVR Vancouver is at operating an airport. We should be grateful that YVR has provided us with such skilled personnel and capitalization to grow our airport to new heights."

Canadian Warplane Heritage Museum

Any visitor to the Canadian Warplane Heritage Museum will be spellbound.

Not only does this "living museum" feature displays of aircraft used by Canadians or Canada's military from World War II to the present, but it also has interactive excitement that overwhelms both young and old.

The museum is, simply, a special place filled with the magic of flight and the mystery of times past.
"Awesome," says one of the entries in the museum guest book.

"Amazing exhibits and very informative," comments another.

The list of accolades goes on. And rightfully so, as the museum leaves no stone unturned as it strives to provide the ultimate unforgettable experience.

Incorporated on December 6, 1971, the museum is located next to the Hamilton International Airport. It began with one aircraft and a dream. Besides its collection of aircraft, the museum has other related aviation artifacts and memorabilia of significant historical importance.

The museum's 108,000-sq. ft. state-of-the-art facility has over 40 aircraft in the collection and some are maintained in flying condition. And it's home to some very unique aircraft; the only operational Avro Lancaster in North America and one of two flying Lancasters in the world, the only operational B-25 'Mitchell' in Canada and the Fleet Fort – the only Canadian-designed and Canadian-built aircraft from WWII that is still flying.

When guests enter the hangar display area they are truly in awe by the size and variety of aircraft that are housed in the museum facility: the entire collection is displayed on one level and it's all under one roof!

The museum utilizes the aircraft display area for special event rentals which can accommodate up to 1,500 people. This unique location also has a variety of meeting rooms available as well as on-site catering. In addition, there is a climate-controlled restaurant serving meals, snacks and beverages.

The museum strives to allow the visitor to experience and interact with the displays. One could climb into the cockpit of a real WWII trainer or a real jet fighter, the Avro CF-100. There are interactive flight combat simulators which will surely test the flight skills of any aspiring aviator. The museum also offers the visitor an educational experience that will take them back through Canadian history. The museum has interactive video displays, movies, photographs and memorabilia from Canadian history.

Visitors should note some of the unique features, such as:

1) Educators can use the museum as an extension of the classroom. Students will learn about teamwork and leadership at our Lancaster Bomber Exhibit. Tours embark on a journey of learning at our living history museum, which features the aircraft used by Canadians or Canadian military from the beginning of WWII to the present. The variety of school-oriented programs are individually designed for all ages and are based on the Ontario Science & Technology and history curriculums. The museum also offers a sleepover program for kids, as well as aircraft modeling programs.

2) Experiencing the thrill of an open cockpit ride in a bi-plane, or a trainer. Treat yourself or that special someone to a ride in a vintage aircraft. Operate a Hawker Hurricane model aircraft: discover the function of rudder, aileron and elevator controls and more. Enjoy a movie in the Rolls-Royce Theatre. Test your aviator skills at interactive displays. Sit in

a C-1119 119 flying boxcar similar. simulator.

3) Seeing aircraft that fly: The museum's collection includes aircraft that fly and several that remain on static display for close-up viewing. A few of the museum's aircraft are interactive displays. See what it's like to sit at the controls of an actual jet aircraft.

4) Plan a special event or business and pleasure. The museums unique aircraft display area is an ideal setting for theme parties, company parties and receptions for up to 1,500 people. If you are planning a business luncheon, meeting or dinner, there are a variety of meeting rooms and event areas available. All catering is prepared on site and the facility is licenced up the LLBO.

5) Guided tours by one of the museum's knowledgeable volunteer visitor services personnel are available.

6) Visit the aviation gift shop and choose from over 300 book titles, hundreds of aviation models, hats, T-shirts, sweatshirts, and unique memorabilia. Then you can relax in the restaurant, open daily for breakfast, lunch or a snack as you look out over Hamilton Airport through floor-to-ceiling windows.

It is important to note that the Canadian Warplane Heritage Museum is a non-profit organization whose mandate is:

1) To acquire, document, preserve and maintain, a complete collection of aircraft that were flown by Canadians and the Canadian military services from the beginning of World War II to the present, including other related aviation artifacts and memorabilia of significant historic importance to this period;

2) To instruct, educate and entertain the general public through the maintenance and rotation of displays, flight demonstration, special events and activities; and encourage Canadians of all ages to become actively involved in the

preservation of these aircraft;

3) To provide facilities for the restoration and protection, interpretation and exhibits of the collection. These will be displayed in their natural element - aerial or static, with emphasis on all aspects of safety and legal obligations in relation to both the artifacts and public; and to deliver programs that meet the standards for community museums in Ontario;

4) And to maintain supportive exhibits to the thousands of men and women who built, serviced and flew these aircraft and in memory of those who did not return.

The museum fulfills its mandate and much, much more. With the exception of Christmas Day and New Year's Day, the museum is open all year round, from 9 a.m. until 5 p.m.

So if you are looking for a real thrill, look no further than the Canadian Warplane Heritage Museum – where history comes alive.

(For complete, up-to-date information about the museum, visit the website at www.warplane.com)

The dramatic entrance way to the Canadian Warplane Heritage Museum. Guided tours by the museum's knowledgeable volunteer visitor services personnel are available.

A majestic view of the Warplaine Heritage Museum, home to the only operational Avro Lancaster in North America and one of two flying Lancasters in the world.

Warplane Heritage Museum guide Bill Tourtel is a valued
source of aviation information at the museum, which
features several unique aircraft and hundreds of displays.

Interior scene at the Warplane Heritage Museum. The
108,000-sq. ft. state-of-the-art facility has over 40 aircraft
in the collection and some are in flying condition.

A familiar statue outside the airport passenger terminal constantly checks his watch to make sure he's not running late. Fortunately, travellers can check through very quickly.

A dramatic sky provides a powerful backdrop to the control tower. More than 600,000 business and pleasure travelers fly from Hamilton on Canada's two leading air carriers.

Richard Koroscil, President/CEO, Hamilton International Airport, now the site of approximately 1,700 jobs as it has grown to become Canada's largest dedicated cargo hub.

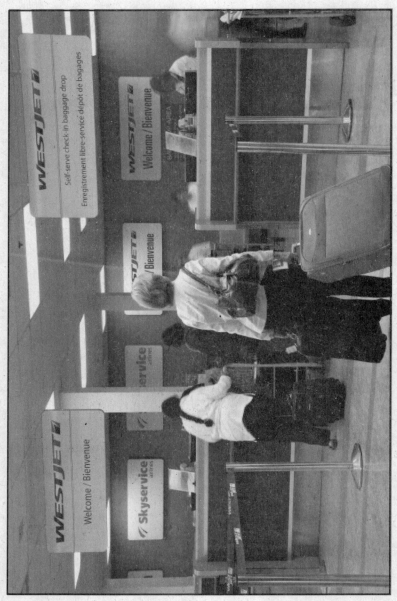

Customers enjoy fast check-through times and service at the WestJet check-in. In sharp contrast to larger airports such as Pearson, Hamilton International is fast, convenient.

Waiting for a flight is a relaxing experience at Hamilton International where customers enjoy a comfortable setting with Internet access. It's the no-worries way to travel.

Celebrating over 10 years in business, WestJet now employs over 6,000 people and has carried over 9.4-million guests. Hamilton remains one of its most important operations.

For fans of great coffee and baked goods, here's a familiar sight that had its origins in Hamilton. Why not take a sip of Hamilton culture? You've always got time for Tim Hortons.

A helpful source of information and ground transportation options can be found just a few steps from the passenger terminal entrance doors.

Ron Foxcroft, TradePort chairman, firmly believes that the airport is providing a substantial boost to Hamilton's profile and is "helping the image of Hamilton," in a big way.

Peninsulair: a familiar presence at the airport. It's Hamilton International's largest training facility.

Another Peninsulair aircraft rests on the tarmac.

A longstanding part of the airport, Glanford Aviation.

Coyote Jack's offers a comfortable place to take a break.

447 Wing has stood the test of time and remains a familiar landmark at the airport.

Avis, Hertz, National - they're all there and ready to serve you at Hamilton International. Seldom has renting a car at an airport been this quick or enjoyable an experience.

Like sentinels standing guard, a trio of gas pumps stand ready to serve.

fly globespan offers convenient, low-cost daily flights to London-Stansted, London-Gatwick, Manchester, Glasgow, Dublin, Shannon Airport, Belfast, Edinburgh, Newcastle, Exeter, Birmingham, Doncaster and Liverpool.

An array of available kiosks adds to the convience and ease of the pleasant air travel experience one always finds at Hamilton International.

A Purolator jet rests on the tarmac at Hamilton International. Purolator, Canada's largest air courier operator, has built its major cross-Canada sort centre at Hamilton.

Jetport was designed and built by a business traveler – Ron
Joyce, the Hamilton billionaire and co-founder of the Tim
Horton's chain – for business executive travellers.

Author Greg McMillan discovered: "Everyone I interviewed had a personal story or a favourite recollection about their experience with the airport."

Cargojet Canada Ltd., operates a network of nine B727-200AF in Canada, providing a premium overnight air cargo service into 12 major city centres throughout Canada.

John Dolbec, chief executive officer of the Hamilton Chamber of Commerce, is a frequent patron of Hamilton International airport as it's "the best," for business and leisure travel.

UPS has invested in a $15-million sort centre at Hamilton International Airport, integrating its cross-Canada and U.S. transborder air cargo shipping.

UPS Canada Ltd.

UPS, the world's largest express carrier, is literally at the "centre" of it all at Hamilton International Airport.

Not only does it have a 47,000-square-foot sort centre onsite, but Hamilton International Airport is also the international hub of Canadian operations for UPS.

UPS Canada Ltd. has scheduled nightly flight operations at Hamilton. These aircrafts consist of one B-757 and two B-727s between the U.S. and Canada. UPS has invested $15-million in the sort centre, integrating its cross-Canada and U.S. transborder air cargo shipping. Domestic services within Canada are performed by All Canada Express, which operates two flights nightly, both all cargo B-727.

UPS Canada first opened for business in the basement of a Toronto hotel on February 28, 1975. Glenn Smith, the company's first president, directed UPS Canada's delivery fleet, which consisted of a single package car delivering in downtown Toronto.

Today, the company has more than 8,000 employees in 54 facilities across the country, and provides service to every address in Canada, the United States, and more than 200 countries and territories worldwide. UPS Canada also plays a key role in the timely and accurate importation and clearance of packages through Canada Customs for all modes of transportation, regardless of whether the shipment is carried by UPS or another carrier.

The UPS Canada headquarters are in Mississauga, Ontario, and other Canadian hubs are in Mirabel, Quebec; Calgary, Alberta; Vancouver, British Columbia; Winnipeg, Manitoba; and Toronto, Ontario. Brokerage operations are headquartered in Fredericton, New Brunswick.

UPS has a long and storied history, beginning in the United States. In 1907 there was a great need in America for private messenger and delivery services. To help meet this need, an enterprising 19-year-old, James E. ("Jim") Casey, borrowed $100 from a friend and established the American Messenger Company in Seattle, Washington. According to accounts given by Jim there were quite a few messenger services already in the Seattle area, some of which he had worked for in the past.

That initial name was well-suited to the business pursuits of the new company. In response to telephone calls received at their basement headquarters, messengers ran errands, delivered packages, and carried notes, baggage, and trays of food from restaurants. They made most deliveries on foot and used bicycles for longer trips. Only a few automobiles were in existence at that time and department stores of the day still used horses and wagons for merchandise delivery. It would be six years before the United States Parcel Post system would be established.

Jim and partner Claude Ryan ran the service from a nondescript office. Jim's brother George and other teens were the company's messengers. The company did well despite stiff competition, largely because of Jim Casey's strict policies of customer courtesy, reliability, round-the-clock service, and low rates. These principles, which guide UPS – United Parcel Service – even today, are summarized by Jim's slogan: Best service and lowest rates.

From those humble beginnings as a messenger company in the U.S., UPS has grown into a $42.6-billion corporation by clearly focusing on the goal of enabling commerce around the globe.

Today, UPS is a global company with one of the most recognized and admired brands in the world. As the largest express carrier and package delivery company in the world, UPS is also a leading provider of specialized transportation, logistics, capital, and e-commerce services. Every day, UPS manages the flow of goods, funds, and information in Canada and more than 200 countries and territories worldwide.

5

You can seek out statistics and you can provide expert analysis.

But, the truth be told, there are no better indicators of economic upsides than good, tried and true real stories from real people.

Such is certainly the case with the impact Hamilton International is having and what it means to the local economy – both now and in the future.

Tyler MacLeod, an investment advisor with Dundas Securities and president of the Hamilton Chamber of Commerce, has an example that perhaps sums up the crucial contribution Hamilton International brings to the table – accessibility.

"I have a friend who runs a publishing and design company," Mr. MacLeod says. "With Hamilton International here, he is able to fly out to clients and fly clients in. That is a tremendous asset.

"It is so important to note that some of the clients might not be clients if this airport did not exist and it was too cumbersome to transact business."

A basic economic need is met. And that story is just the tip of the iceberg.

Wherever you look, you find valid and impressive information that shows just how valuable Hamilton International is to the Hamilton and Greater Golden Horseshoe economies.

In its economic development review for 2007, the city of Hamilton dedicated an entire section to Hamilton International.

Said the report: "Hamilton International (hi) epitomizes the secondary airport profile: competitive passenger carrier service, low airport fees, quick aircraft turnaround, no congestion and convenient low-cost parking. The airport's mission and strategy is to always stay tactically ahead of the needs and wants of its passengers. Hamilton International is a solutions provider and continues to stay both service-oriented and cost-effective."

The report went on to say: "A milestone saw Hamilton International officially operating with a CAT II Instrument Landing System ... maximizes the airport's ability to increase accessibility during inclement weather conditions and reduce landing limits on its 10,000-foot runway.

"The announcement of a $1.6-million expansion to the international arrivals area will accommodate hi's growing transborder and international business and customers."

And the report continued with glowing comments about Hamilton International's role as Canada's largest courier and cargo airport: "It is home to four of the major cargo/courier companies: Cargojet, DHL, UPS and Purolator and generates more dedicated cargo flights than any other airport in Canda.

"Cargo highlights for 2006 saw Cargojet increase flights by 30 per cent, which included bringing in BAX Global, a principal transportation and logistics service provider, to Hamilton International from Toronto. UPS also doubled its Hamilton flight schedule.

"Partnered with the city of Hamilton's economic

development division, Hamilton International had the opportunity to showcase its cargo operations to the world with a special presentation during the Air Cargo Forum, the industry's leading event, in Calgary."

More telling positive economic signs came to light with another city of Hamilton study conducted in 2005, entitled Hamilton Goods Movements.

The most intriguing components dealt with the vision for the future. An excerpt from the study explains in more detail:

"How will [economic] success be recognized?
There are many diverse aspects covered in the scope of this study and there are many fields of action. Yet there is the need for an over-arching visionary statement that helps all participants maintain sight of a goal and stay on course. Following are some statements that attempt to articulate at a high level, what the future might contain. These are generally drawn from study participants and the stakeholder consultations.

Short Term – 1-5 Years:

All land use planning decisions adequately consider direct and indirect impact on the ability for businesses to move goods and acknowledge the critical importance of supporting and promoting industry as the major generator of employment in Hamilton.

The Aerotropolis cluster is established. The port multi-modal logistics cluster land assembly is advanced, and planning for new facilities and services is well into the approvals stage.

The city of Hamilton is an advocate for the goods movement industry and is demonstrating this by implementing local roadway improvements, more goods-specific signage and taking an active role in the Southern Ontario Gateway Council.

Programs to prepare the workforce to respond to existing and future job opportunities in goods movement and related fields are being implemented by governments, educators and industryworking together.

Medium Term – 5-10 Years

Industries that rely on just-in-time delivery are moving to Hamilton to take advantage of the availability of 24-hour operations at air, marine and intermodal facilities, placing Hamilton at an advantage compared to its neighbours. Sufficiently large employment lands are assembled, serviced and ready for these new industries comprising a variety of economic clusters.

The Aerotropolis cluster has one or two new key establishments; traffic and employment growth outpace the growth of the economy. The port multimodal logistics cluster is established and contributing to growth in employment. Other clusters are also evolving in line with the city's economic development strategy.

Certification programs are generating graduates to fill new job opportunities and continuing education is also established to keep the work force prepared to meet new challenges.

Long Term – 10-15 Years:

Hamilton is benefitting to full advantage from its transportation network and strategic location which enable goods movement providers, industry and businesses exploit the many cost and time effective transportation modes available while minimizing energy costs and supporting environmental goals.

The continuing growth in employment, quality of life and excellence of service make Hamilton a shining example of "best practice" that others attempt to emulate. It enjoys a key role in logistics and distribution of raw materials and finished goods in North America."

Mr. MacLeod sees many direct positive effects that can be attributed to Hamilton International.

"The airport provides vital links to the rest of Canada and the world, for that matter," he said. "Both passenger and freight service allow Hamilton to compete internationally, not just regionally and nationally. This access is crucial in today's world and the airport can help our city capture recognition as a destination and transportation hub that is world class.

"The economic effects can be looked at both indirectly and directly. The fact that we have a growing airport enables local industry and business to increase their profile, and the city as well, as an accessible destination.

"Travelers and goods are able to 'knock on our front door' so to speak. It is a great thing to have the ability to fly guests or business representatives directly to our great city. The direct impact is employment, through receipt of goods and transshipment. Goods can leave directly from their processing and manufacture areas here in Hamilton saving excess shipping costs. Also there is the actual onsite jobs the airport can provide. Couple that with tourism and you get a pretty winning scenario.

"As the president of the Hamilton Chamber of Commerce, I feel the airport is a positive economic driver for the city. That is our focus, as the voice of business. I see multiple and far reaching positives for many aspects of our business community. Also, as an investment advisor, I see many, many businesses that rely on transportation for goods\ services\people all the time. We are able to capitalize and attract those types of business."

And all indications are that the economic boost will continue, in effect guaranteeing that not only Hamilton International will be Flying High.

Hamilton Chamber of Commerce:
Business leadership for an expanding economy

Hamilton International Airport is without question a powerful catalyst for growth and development throughout the Hamilton region. That's the consensus of business leaders and politicians at every level of government.

Yet the airport's full potential as a generator of jobs and prosperity is being compromised by overly cautious approaches to development, asserts John Dolbec, chief executive officer for the Hamilton Chamber of Commerce.

Mr. Dolbec notes that while brownfields – vacated pre-industrialized lands – are often touted at the preferred development option, such land parcels are often too small for most light industrial developers who seek parcel's of five acres or more to accommodate factories, warehouses, parking and shipping lanes.

"The airport lands are about the last area in Hamilton where adequate parcels of land can be found," Mr. Dolbec observes, adding that it's important that such lands, if allowed to be developed, be restricted to light industrial only and not given over to suburban sprawl.

Mr. Dolbec says the airport's full potential as a generator of jobs and growth can best be realized if surrounding lands are allowed to develop, creating employment and prosperity in the process.

He notes the airport is already one of the busiest facilities in Canada for cargo freight and has the potential to become a major international airport for passenger travel. Direct and indirect employment from support businesses and other commercial enterprises could also add tens of thousands of new jobs.

A number of studies, including Vision 2020 and Places to Grow predict continued population growth with some forecasts calling for as many as 4 million more people will move into the Hamilton-centred Golden Horseshoe in the next 30 years. Studies also indicate the Hamilton region will deplete all remaining space in its existing light industrial parks and will need another 1,000 hectares to accommodate growth during this time-span and most of this needed land can be found in 850 hectares around Hamilton International – although its current status as farmland has made this issue highly controversial.

Mr. Dolbec says studies estimate developing the airport lands could generate 50,000 jobs – or more – and provide a significant degree of sustainable prosperity to the region.

Of course, land development is only one component of a healthy Hamilton area economy. Mr. Dolbec also points to ongoing downtown revitalization efforts; an expanding education sector with expansions to McMaster University and Mohawk College; a growing health care sector and a steadily diversifying economy that continues to move away from the predominantly heavy industrial model of the now distant past.

Achieving business success in the Hamilton market is made much easier and is accomplished in a more efficient manner through business community networking, an area Mr. Dolbec and the Chamber specialize in.

Clearly, Businesses serious about success rely on a key organization for help: the Hamilton Chamber of Commerce. Indeed, the Chamber's slogan: "Creating Business Opportunities," speaks to the services it's provided for more than 160 years.

Chamber-created business opportunities include frequent chances to network.: Members are provided with a number of catered business forums – most of them free of charge – throughout the year to promote their goods and services to 1,700 fellow Chamber members.

But the opportunities don't end there. As Mr. Dolbec notes: "The benefits are extensive – what you get out of the

Chamber depends, in part, in what you happen to put into it."

"We have numerous breakfast meetings, special events and committees you can get involved with, and your involvement can bring you a good deal of insight and information on a range of topics," Mr. Dolbec adds in an interview at Chamber headquarters, at the foot of Bay Street in a building shared with the Royal Hamilton Yacht Club.

"Each Chamber member has an individual reason for joining the organization and we attempt to respond to those needs as individually as possible," Mr. Dolbec says, rising from his chair to savour an enviable view of ducks and sailboats gliding serenely on calm recreational waters that shimmer in the sun.

"The mission of the Chamber as the voice of ethical enterprise is that we are committed to making Hamilton a great place to live, work, play and invest, while recognizing the importance of the individual as the most significant contributor to achieving community objectives."

The Chamber's ongoing success is pegged to its central role in fostering the growth of Hamilton's traditional role as a major commercial centre.

Indeed, from very early in its history, before steel and heavy industry, Hamilton was a thriving centre of trade and commerce – a proud heritage that continues through to this day.

In fact, in 1845 – a year before the Hamilton community was duly incorporated as the City of Hamilton – the bustling community had by that point already established the Hamilton Board of Trade, the business-promoting forerunner of today's Hamilton Chamber of Commerce. And the importance of business people in making a difference wasn't lost on the board's first-ever president, Isaac Buchanan, a visionary who noted back in 1845 "without the committed leadership of those who strive to build an economy, our community will cease to strengthen and grow."

As well, the Hamilton Board of Trade had been an early supporter of free trade with the United States, although it reversed that position in 1910 to an effort to protect Hamilton manufacturers. Almost 80 years later the chamber would again support free trade with the Americans, indeed the world at large.

In 1903, the board pushed for civic improvements such as additional drinking fountains. It also formed an alliance with Hamilton's Trades and Labour Council to arbitrate an end to a costly Teamsters strike hurting the local economy.

And in 1920 another milestone was reached when the board reconstituted itself as the Hamilton Chamber of Commerce and quickly took on such successful projects as relocating McMaster University from Toronto to Hamilton and helping establish the Chedoke Golf Course.

During the Great Depression of the 1930s, the chamber demonstrated considerable compassion for the less fortunate members of Hamilton society. The chamber initiated a system of garden plots allowing the unemployed to grow produce. And it raised funds to cover rent owed by needy citizens.

From 1939-1945, the chamber supported the Second World War effort by organizing massive donations of foodstuffs and gifts for the City of Hamilton Tiger Squadron, a bomber squadron manned by local volunteers fighting overseas.

As Hamilton celebrated its centennial in 1946, the chamber played its usual active role, promoting, among other major events, the first Miss Canada Pageant.

During the 1980s, the chamber could be found supporting the Corporate Challenge fitness and fun event, Crime Stoppers and a Chinese chamber to attract Asian investment.

In the 1990s, the chamber continued its active role, speaking out on tax issues, government budgets and legislative concerns while bringing a lengthy list of prominent business leaders and speakers to the city to address everything from business strategies for success to exports and international trade.

During the 1996 Hamilton Sesquicentennial year, the chamber contributed enormously to making it a very successful year. Among the Chamber's many achievements was the introduction of a striking commemorative Sesquicentennial coin created by Ancaster sculptor Elizabeth Holbrook.

Also in the mid-1990s, the Globe & Mail's Report on Business magazine ranked the Hamilton area as one of the best communities in which one can do business in Canada. Clearly the Hamilton Chamber's oft-said message – that Hamilton is a great place to do business – seems to finally be getting out to the national media.

The need to repeat this message to wider audiences has been taken to heart by the chamber's many members who play a leadership role in building our economic region. And this historic role is now being championed by a new generation of chamber members, many of them young entrepreneurs and small business people.

Mr. Dolbec also notes the Chamber has experienced first-hand the rise of small businesses as the Canadian economy's leading source of new jobs and opportunities.

"An overwhelming number of our members are small businesses," he acknowledges.

"At one time the major industries accounted for the bulk of jobs, but that's changed," he adds. "Small businesses are where you'll find the most employment growth. There are more small businesses around today than ever before – and that's certainly reflected in our membership. The trend started in the mid-1990s and has continued to this day."

Mr. Dolbec remarks that the mid-1990s was also when the Chamber began targeting small businesses by starting programs that catered to one-man outfits to small firms with 100 or fewer employees.

In fact, Mr. Dolbec observes that most of the growth in manufacturing jobs has occurred outside the steel industry via an abundance of small manufacturers each employing fewer than 100 people. "We're also seeing growth in services in general, high tech industries, bio-technology jobs and information services," he adds. "And entrepreneurs are creating many of these new jobs. People getting into business on their own are creating their own job plus additional jobs for other people."

Small businesses, including home-based businesses, now constitute the fastest growing source of members at the chamber and this has led the organization to devote more time and energy representing the concerns of small business.

That change in approach reflects a societal reality: Small businesses dominate the new age economy.

Mr. Dolbec observes that small business remains the primary source of new jobs "and that's probably a good thing. It would seem to be healthier to depend on many small companies for jobs than rely on one or two big firms to create employment."

He says that with growing numbers of entrepreneurs and small businesses starting up and thriving, the economy is becoming more and more diverse.

"Diversity is a real strength. You're not as dependent on one or two sectors of the economy or one or two companies to keep you going. Economic changes that hurt some companies may not hurt others. Having a diversified economy means you're in a better position to withstand an inevitable recession."

Yet Mr. Dolbec also observes that diversity is just one of the competitive advantages enjoyed by the Greater

Hamilton area. "Some of our other strengths include the ability of many of our companies to make specialized products and services for niche markets," he notes.

"When you look at all of our strengths, it's apparent that we're well-positioned to weather economic downturns and thrive in economic recoveries."

One component of Hamilton's diversified economy is its vibrant transportation section, including the busiest port in the St. Lawrence Seaway system, and an airport that continues to grow and expand.

"What's happening at the airport has just been phenomenal – it's frequently listed as the number one airport in Canada for freight," Mr. Dolbec asserts.

Mr. Dolbec notes the Chamber and the city of Hamilton have always been inextricably tied to one another. "The chamber has always been front and centre when it comes to addressing the legitimate concerns of business and the community. Our history and our future are closely tied to making our business community – and the wider community beyond that – as successful as possible."

Mr. Dolbec notes that visitors to Hamilton are often struck by how attractive the city is. Its vistas, parks and pleasant neighbourhoods can quickly dispel any lingering, outdated images of Hamilton as a gritty centre of heavy industry.

Yes, the city remains proud of its heavy industrial heritage, prouder still that it remains home to many heavy and light industries.

And Canada's Steel City is more than a little proud that it's home to the nation's two largest steelmakers, Stelco Inc. and Dofasco Inc.

Many millions of dollars in technology investments have made the steel giants efficient, high tech companies that produce more tons of steel per man-hour than most of their rivals.

Yet, while the steel industry and support industries remain a major source of employment in Hamilton, the city's economy has steadily diversified over the years. The health care services sector now employs more people in Hamilton than any other sector.

And Hamilton is one of the most livable cities in the world, boasting an abundance of parks, many festivals, a recreational waterfront, relatively little traffic congestion, less pollution than many other major cities, low unemployment, affordable housing and an overall quality of life that is the envy of many communities.

By the late 1990s, the population of the former Hamilton-Wentworth region approached 470,000 people – more than 320,000 of them residing in Hamilton itself.

And by 2002, following the amalgamation of Hamilton and Wentworth as the single City of Hamilton, the total population exceeded 500,000 people – all of them residing in the now expanded city. Hamilton was a full-fledged metropolis of more than half-a-million people – and growing fast.

Add in th

e interdependent, interconnected regions of Halton and Niagara and it's apparent Hamilton is the economic and geographic hub of an economic region of more than 1 million people.

The borders of this vast economic region are also somewhat elastic and can include Hamilton-Norfolk lands to the south, Grimsby to the east and Brant County to the west, increasing the population to more than 1.2 million.

Hamilton is at the heart of a community of communities, a Hamilton-centred hinterland of shared geography and economic interests.

And this economic region boasts a highly diversified economy, including everything from soft fruit growing and winemaking, to heavy industry and high tech companies.

107

The chamber is now focusing on how Hamilton can best take advantage of its enviable position at the hub of one of North America's most densely populated international markets. Within a 500-mile radius of Hamilton, about a day's truck drive, is a total market population of 120 million people. "People are beginning to get the message that, as proud as we are of our steel industry, there's a lot more to Hamilton than steel," Mr. Dolbec notes.

Just a few years ago, Hamilton companies exported more than 50 per cent of the goods and services produced in this city. Today, exports account for fully two-thirds of local output, with most of these goods and services bound for the United States.

"The U.S. is the biggest recipient of our exports," Mr. Dolbec observes. "There's a huge amount of cross border trade that takes place here."

Brownfields, vacated or underused lands that once housed industries, are giving rise to new companies and new sources of employment. One of the most striking examples of a brownfield being transformed into a bustling centre of commerce can be found on Hamilton's industrialized waterfront. An entire community of small businesses has now found a home in old, previously vacated factories and warehouses that once were used by industrial giants. This industrial park space is now being leased by the Hamilton Harbour Commissioners at low rental rates to an array of tenants, including De Feo's Auto Service Ltd., which has expanded to include several adjoining service bays in a former industrial warehouse. Numerous other businesses have long made their home in the immediate area, including McKeil marine and Heddle Marine.

The information age economy is also bringing new job opportunities. Fibre optic wire firms have made the downtown core a leader among inner city cores for its ability to offer high-speed Internet even in old buildings. This growth has also meant hundreds of jobs.

Efforts are also underway to develop Hamilton's 'smart community' potential, via uplinks to satellite linkages, allowing doctors many miles apart to have a fibre optic consultation on television screens. A diagnosis or patient information can be shared instantly via multimedia, telecommunication uplink technology.

That such dynamic endeavours would locate in downtown Hamilton shouldn't be surprising. The city's core boasts an abundance of available space at relatively low rates. Although still struggling in places, Hamilton's downtown is seeing many millions of dollars in investment. "There are great opportunities downtown," Mr. Dolbec notes. "The realty prices are low, the problems are solvable and the potential is great."

Mr. Dolbec also observes the community has become a well-organized whole with once-distant institutions regularly conferring with each other to devise programs that can best exploit the new commercial and employment opportunities a changing business world is offering. The Chamber is in regular contact with the Hamilton Economic Development Department, Mohawk College, McMaster University and HIT (Hamilton Incubator for Technology), which serves as an incubator for start-up high-tech firms.

Mr. Dolbec points out that the Chamber worked closely with Hamilton's Economic Development Department in the drafting of a new strategic plan to guide the city into a prosperous future of growth. "It's a very co-operative relationship," Mr. Dolbec notes. There's a common desire to work together to solve our problems and help our community prosper. And there's a very strong sense of everyone working together to face common challenges – you don't find that in very many communities."

"In fact," he continues, "one of the really beautiful things I love about Hamilton is that this is a very close-knit community. There's a lot of warm-hearted, generous people who don't hesitate to roll up their sleeves and work together to help the community prosper and grow."

Not that there aren't problems. "We're frequently faced with shortages of skilled labour," Mr. Dolbec notes. "Anyone with marketable skills – particularly skilled trades people such as tool and die makers, electricians, carpenters and machinists - are finding it relatively easy to find work."

Mr. Dolbec notes many skilled trades people are middle-aged or older and there is no new generation of skilled trades to replace them. "The demand for new skilled trades people is there – the supply isn't. It's important that we find ways, develop programs, to create the skills that are needed in our community. It's unfortunate that some firms are losing business because they lack skilled trades people and the jobs are going begging."

Mr. Dolbec says the Ontario-wide shortage of skilled trades presents a huge opportunity for those people willing to learn a trade. "Unfortunately, not many young people are eager to get into the trades. There seems to be a stigma about working with your hands, despite the fact that many of these jobs have well paying starting salaries."

He says Europe's strengthening economies have made immigration less of a solution than ever to the skilled trades shortage. "Business hasn't done enough to train future generations – it's coming back to haunt us," he adds.

"However, there are genuine efforts underway to address this problem. Businesses are working closely with community colleges to create and promote programs to create the skills."

Mr. Dolbec takes heart in the work being done to ensure a new generation has the option of going into a trade. "There's more of a willingness and effort to address these problems than there perhaps has been in some time."

He says Hamilton's favourable position is owed in

part to it geographical location in the huge Southern Ontario market with access to the even greater U.S. market.

He says both the Canada-U.S. Free Trade Agreement and the subsequent North American Free Trade Agreement have truly succeeded in giving Hamilton companies relatively unfettered access to the American market.

"There were concerns from some that free trade would cost jobs. What we've found instead is that free trade has saved jobs and created jobs."

To become part of this success story, Mr. Dolbec advises joining the Hamilton Chamber of Commerce; participating in as many chamber activities and events as possible, networking; handing out business cards; and tapping into the expertise of fellow chamber members.

Mr. Dolbec also notes the city's entire economy has diversified. After years of downsizing, the big industries seem to have found an employment balance and they remain a secure source of existing jobs. The Manufacturing sector is vibrant, the health care and education sectors are growing and the entire services sector is expanding. Hamilton still boasts one of the lowest unemployment rates in all of Canada as one advantage among many. "We have low unemployment rates, a highly skilled labour force, a great quality of life and, compared to many other centres, the cost of doing business here is low. We also offer fast, convenient access to markets in Toronto and the U.S."

"In every area you can think of, Hamilton continues to provide an enviable place to live, work and play."

Contact information for Hamilton Chamber of Commerce:
555 Bay St. N., Hamilton, Ontario L8L 1H1
Phone: (905) 522-1151
Fax: (905) 522-1154
E-Mail: hdcc@ hamiltonchamber.on.ca
Web: www.hamiltonchamber.on.ca

Clarence and Leonard Bick with Brian Johnson, Bernice
Cairns, John Knechtel and George Van Arragon at Bick
Financial Security in Ancaster.

Bick Financial Security:
Managing the future for a growing clientele

Greater numbers of people are moving into the Hamilton area, thanks in part to the economic growth and convenient air travel offered by Hamilton International airport. The expanding population has increased the need for financial services, in particular, financial planning.

While the sector as a whole has grown, some firms, such as Bick Financial Security have found it necessary to accommodate growth through the addition of more offices in more communities, and the Bick Financial Security story is illustrative of the growth occurring in the entire financial services sector.

Brothers Leonard and Clarence Bick grew up in Ancaster and later attended nearby McMaster University where they each earned MBAs in the early 1980s. They also hold CFP (Certified Financial Planner) and RFP (Registered Financial Planner) certifications. In 1987, the Bick brothers already had several years financial planning experience when they became managers of the Hamilton offices of Financial Concept Group.

Then, in 1993, they took over the Ancaster FCG offices and founded the Bick Financial Security firm. After starting out as a small firm, Bick Financial Security Corporation today has several office locations that together provide financial planning and independent brokerage services to more than 4,000 individuals, families and businesses. The company now has more than half-a-billion dollars in assets under administration.

Bick Financial Security is constantly reaching out to new prospective clients to fill a need far too many people still overlook. Many people still devote little time to one of life's most important issues: Their own financial security.

113

Surveys suggest most Canadians will spend more time watching TV in an evening than they'll spend on financial planning in a whole year. Although few would argue against the importance of building financial security, life's more trivial matters easily distract us. Often, financial planning seems to be a matter that we'd rather not consider.

Fortunately, the subject of building a secure financial future garners a lot of thoughtful consideration at Bick Financial Security Corporation.

"We spend a lot of time on long-term portfolio planning and keeping current with investment products," notes Leonard Bick, a managing partner with the Ancaster-based firm.

"Our mission is to help clients achieve financial security," he adds in an interview at the company's office in a stone building on Wilson Street.

Mr. Bick, 52, notes most people are happy to let a professional plan out their financial future while they get on with their day-to-day lives. Even those rare individuals who take a strong interest and prefer to do their own financial planning can find the task daunting, observes Mr. Bick, who, with older brother Clarence, 53, is a principal in the firm.

"Our clients are becoming more sophisticated and knowledgeable, but the rate of change goes beyond the ability of most people to keep pace," Len Bick notes. "Even for those of us in the business, staying current with all of the changes can be a challenge, but we work very hard at keeping up."

To tailor a Financial Plan to a client's needs, a six-step financial planning process is followed that includes: assessing the client's situation; establishing client goals, priorities and concerns; identifying problems and opportunities; providing written recommendations and alternative solutions; taking action on implementation; and, doing periodic reviews, updates and revisions to the Plan.

"You are as special and unique as your personal financial goals and situation," Mr. Bick explains. "At Bick Financial, we discuss those goals and invest safely and profitably to achieve them. We then monitor results with regular reviews."

"To keep you informed , we provide newsletters, and timely market commentaries, a financial library, investment awareness kits, regular investment seminars and workshops," adds Mr. Bick, whose Ancaster head office is located in a homey heritage building in Ancaster where you'll find excellent service, free parking and fresh coffee. There are also offices in Grimsby, Milton, Smithville, St. Catharines, Stoney Creek, and Toronto.

The personal, professional approach has earned Bick Financial Security several top Readers' Choice awards for best financial planner in the area media, including The Hamilton Spectator and St. Catharines Standard. The firm has also named a finalist by the Hamilton Chamber of Commerce in its annual Outstanding Business Achievement Awards honoring businesses that have demonstrated excellence in a variety of areas, including entrepreneurship, employee relations, business achievement, community relations and innovation.

Such accolades are much deserved by Bick Financial Securities 15 financial advisors, who offer a wealth of knowledge from professional backgrounds including accounting, education, finance and business.

And a team of 30 experienced staff supports the advisors and their clients. But, more importantly, the advisors at Bick Financial understand that the most important aspect of the business is to know the clients.

Joining the Bicks are fellow financial planners Bernice Cairns, a certified management accountant; George Van Arragon; Brian Johnson; and Dr. John Knechtel. Financial planner Melissa DeBrouwer heads the firm's Milton office.

All of these financial planners take a conservative approach to building wealth on behalf of clients. Investment strategies tend to be long-term. But each client's financial plan is tailored to meet his or her specific needs. One of Bick Financial Security's strengths is that it's an independent company that is not tied to a particular mutual fund. This means the financial advisors are free to search out the best products from more than 1,000 of the top mutual funds on the market.

They can also choose the most promising GICs (Guaranteed Investment Certificates) from 30 trust companies and select from a variety of other investment devices such as segregated funds, bonds and labour sponsored investment funds, providing the ability to achieve a product mix most suited to the client's needs. Assisting the financial planners and their clients is a support staff of 21.

Another great strength at Bick Financial is the company's community ties. The advisors live in the communities they service, sponsor several local youth sports teams and are members of several service clubs, including Rotary and the Ancaster division of the Hamilton and District Chamber of Commerce.

Their Wilson Street building is also a local landmark and is a recognized part of Ancaster's architectural heritage. Known historically as the Carriage Works, the building had been used since the 1860s to build horse-drawn carriages. In 1885, the existing stone structure was built on the foundations of the original building after it was destroyed in a fire.

Professional financial planning takes a holistic approach to an individual's financial life. A qualified Bick Financial planner will consider a client's goals, stage in life, personal circumstances and risk tolerance. They will make recommendations for growing and preserving wealth, minimizing tax, estate planning, insurance – and more, depending on the individual they are working with. In some cases, this same professional will be involved in executing some of the recommendations (e.g. sell specific products). In other cases, these transactions will be done separately with other professionals. A Bick Advisor will obtain information about your financial resources and obligations through interviews or questionnaires and gather all the necessary documents before giving you the advice you need. Then, you and your advisor will define your personal and financial goals, needs and priorities; investigate your values, preferences, financial outlook and desired results as they relate to your financial goals, needs and priorities; and develop a financial plan tailored to meet your goals and objectives, values, temperament and risk tolerance, along with projections and recommendations.

A common element to most financial plans is the inclusion of RRSPs or registered retirement savings plans that allow Canadians to save for retirement and achieve tax breaks in the process.

"The RRSP is really nothing more than a special kind of box," Mr. Bick Explains. "It's designed to hold tax-deductible investments in a registered account so they can build tax-free until they're withdrawn. You can have as many RRSPs as you want, although it's better to have fewer for ease of management and to minimize any fees. Since contributions are tax-deductible, they'll be more valuable to those with higher incomes. Once inside the tax-sheltered environment, the investments can grow faster than they would outside an RRSP, where they would face tax on their gains. You can invest in a wide variety of investments - cash, GICs, mutual funds, bonds, exchange-traded funds mortgage-backed securities, stocks, labour-sponsored funds, and income trusts that invest in everything from oil and gas to peat moss and real estate. Up to 30 per cent of the money you invest can be put into foreign investments."

"You can continue to contribute to an RRSP until the

end of the year in which you turn 69," he adds, "provided you still have earned income. At that time, you must convert your RRSP into a Registered Retirement Income Fund, buy an annuity, or withdraw it in cash (generally not a good idea as you'll pay tax on the whole amount and won't have a retirement income). As to what you should invest in, consult a financial adviser. If you don't have a company pension plan, you may want to be more conservative. If you're not far from retirement, you may also want to be more conservative. The choice is yours. Be sure you know what your risk tolerance is."

While there seems to be enormous pressure for everyone to contribute to RRSPs, there may well be a better use for your money, Mr. Bick observes. "For those with a lot of high-interest credit card debt, it may be better to pay that off first," he suggests.

How much will you pay in income taxes over your working life? The professional at Bick Financial can help you reduce that amount through a number of options, such as income-splitting; capital gains and losses; and the types of investments you buy and the income they produce. A Bick Financial Security advisor can help guide you through such options and also advise on ways you can make your mortgage tax deductible and choose the right mutual funds.

"To be a successful investor you don't need $75,000, years of experience, subscriptions to the best investing newsletters, and the time to read them - all you need is a good mutual fund manager," Mr. Bick notes.

"Mutual funds are composed of investors just like you who have mutually decided to pool their money and hire a professional investment manager," he adds.

"You don't even have to round up all your friends and convince them to invest with you. Existing mutual funds are offered by investment companies, banks, trust companies, credit unions, insurance companies, even professional organizations. Mutual funds offer professional management and investment diversification. By not centralizing all your funds in one specific investment, you reduce your risks while increasing the possibility of gains. Because mutual funds are generally regarded as long-term investments, you don't have to worry about them daily."

"Mutual funds have differing objectives," he concludes. "Some may concentrate on speculative growth investments, others on preservation of capital and a steady income. The trick is to find a fund which shares your objectives. Mutual fund portfolios may include common stocks, preferred shares, bonds, treasury bills, precious metals, and real estate in any combination. Day-to-day investment decisions are made by the fund manager who decides the asset mix within the objectives of the fund."

Professional management, diversification, and long-term gains are the benefits of mutual funds. Your Bick Financial advisor can advise you on which mutual funds are best for you and your investment goals.

Having an up-to-date Estate Plan with a valid Will helps to ensure that your dependents and heirs will be provided for according to your wishes. It can also help reduce or defer taxes and provide other benefits – and here again a Bick advisor can help.

Mr. Bick says the company may well expand its branch offices but remains committed to Ancaster.

"This is our home town and it's where we want to be. Instead of spending hours commuting – we'd rather spend that time on our clients."

Contact information for Bick Financial Security Corporation:
241 Wilson Street East, Ancaster, Ontario, L9G 2B8
Phone: (905) 648-9559   Fax: (905) 648-8185
Toll free: 1-888-RSP-BICK (1-888-777-2425)
Email: bettencourt@bickfinancial.com

Ken Lindsay / Mortgage Financial:
Home ownership help for a growing population

As Hamilton International airport continues to act as a magnet, attracting an influx of upwardly mobile people, the growing Hamilton area population's demand for housing is accelerating. Yet, for too many people, the dream of home ownership remains nothing more than a dream. Ken Lindsay makes that dream a reality.

Mr. Lindsay, 44, is a mortgage broker: He shops the market for the best mortgage deals he can find his clients – even those with financial and credit rating issues.

"We specialize in serving the local market – and it's a growing market – and we take pride in generating savings to the customer," notes Mr. Lindsay, president of Mortgage Financial Corporation.

Mr. Lindsay heads the highly successful mortgage broker firm and shops the market to find the best possible mortgages for clients. He puts together mortgages that best meet a client's needs. His firm has grown steadily over the years and now provides employment for several brokers plus support staff. It's now one of the largest independent mortgage brokers in south-western Ontario and also boasts a thriving Brantford office.

"Whether the client is financially successful or is currently facing financial issues, we can save them some money by shopping the mortgage market to find a deal that best meets their needs," he explains in an interview at company headquarters on Ray Street South, Hamilton.

"There aren't too many people who can go to a bank on their own and get a better deal than we can, generally," Mr. Lindsay asserts. "That's because we're also able to exercise a fair amount of buying power, some real financial clout, given the amount of business we bring to the banks," adds

121

Mr. Lindsay, very much a hands-on broker who continues to personally arrange mortgages on behalf of his many clients.

"And for those customers who have been turned down by a bank, we're often able to get them a mortgage – sometimes from the same bank that turned them down – by negotiating a deal that works for everyone," adds Mr. Lindsay whose company arranges several millions of dollars worth of mortgages annually and is enjoying 30 per cent annual growth partly due to the airport's role in bringing new people into the Hamilton region.

Financial lenders, including banks and trust companies, pay the firm a finder's fee/commission for bringing them ready-to-go mortgage deals involving financially secure borrowers.

The arrangement also works well for banks, which rely on the broker to bring them mortgage business. As well, the bank gets to sit back while the broker does the bulk of the work. And the bank will withhold any commission until the successful completion of a mortgage deal. "It's basically a risk-free undertaking for the banks – it's really good for all of the financial institutions," Mr. Lindsay notes, "and the banks remain suppliers of the mortgage funds in most cases."

And for would-be homeowners who have credit difficulties and have been turned down by the banks, there is still hope. Mortgage Financial charges a fee to these less-secure clients to arrange a mortgage on their behalf, normally at somewhat higher interest rates to reflect the added degree of risk involved. "Usually we can negotiate a deal at virtually no cost to the mortgage-borrower – they literally have nothing to lose and everything to gain with lower rates and better terms," Mr. Lindsay says, noting these clients account for 75 per cent of his business, "and we can sometimes even beat the rates the banks offer their own staff."

"Even for the clients who are not financially secure, we can often put together a deal that's not a whole lot more expensive than what someone in a more financially advantageous position would be taking on," he adds.

"It comes down to the volume of business we do – it's buying power," explains the amiable broker, who resides in Ancaster with his wife Monica and children Max, 12, and nine-year-old twins Brad and Jeff.

Even a modest difference in interest rates can prove substantial. For example, before factoring in property taxes, a $100,000 mortgage, amortized over 20 years (the full lifespan of the mortgage) at a 3 per cent interest rate would cost the borrower $554 in monthly principal-and-interest payments. But the same mortgage with a 4 percent interest rate would push the monthly payments to more than $600. And at 5 per cent, the monthly payment needed increases to $660. A further increase of less than one per cent – to 5.75 per cent – inflates the monthly payments to a still more costly $700. Mortgage Financial broker-agents routinely save their clients many thousands of dollars in mortgage payments annually by arranging lower-rate mortgages.

"We can benefit the customer, whether they're well-off or have financial concerns by shopping the market on their behalf to get the best mortgage possible for them at the best terms and rates," Mr. Lindsay asserts.

"If they're financially well-off, we can get them better rates and better terms than they'll likely be able to get on their own," adds Mr. Lindsay, whose company puts together several thousand mortgages a year – worth over $100-million, generates over $3-million in revenue and is experiencing annual growth of 30 per cent.

"And, if the client is struggling a little or working through some financial issues, we can, in most cases, get them a pretty good mortgage when they otherwise might not be able to get any mortgage at all," he adds.

"The secret of our success is getting into the minds of the clients and getting the detailed information we need to help them," Mr. Lindsay asserts, noting that his team is becoming more knowledgeable and skilled. "It's our job to know what people need – not the customer's job to find out – we're valued for our opinion and expertise; it's our job."

Mr. Lindsay notes that bank turn-downs account for 10 to 15 per cent of business and turning these deals around often involves creatively thinking outside the box to structure deals with co-signers or other arrangements that reduce risk and make banks more likely to lend funds.

More and more Canadians are coming to see the inherent value of arranging mortgages through a broker, but in Canada the percentage of people taking this route is just 35 per cent, well behind the U.S. rate of 85 per cent.

Mr. Lindsay's Mortgage Financial firm is today one of the largest independent mortgage brokers in south-western Ontario, with business volume in the tens of millions of dollars. How he rose to become a leading mortgage broker and highly successful businessman is a story that begins in the city of Brantford, a city only recently coming back from years of hard times and failed industries. In the midst of economic devastation, too many local citizens adopted a "no you can't" attitude toward success. Yet, it was in this oft-times negative civic atmosphere and outlook that a young Ken Lindsay's entrepreneurial spirit would emerge.

"I think I've always wanted to succeed in a business of some kind," Mr. Lindsay recalls. Driven by a desire to achieve, he left Brantford for Hamilton in 1982 where he attended McMaster University and completed a Bachelor of Economics (B.Econ) degree in 1986. After graduating, he began working as a salesman in Toronto for the 3M company, selling business equipment, including fax machines to corporate customers.

During his first year out of university, Lindsay invested some of his 3M salesman earnings into the purchase both halves of a two-family, semi-detached duplex house in Hamilton's leafy Westdale community – the home of McMaster University – which he then rented out as student housing. The experience of buying up real estate provided Lindsay with some personal experience of what it means to obtain and maintain mortgages.

It also taught him location and timing are everything. "Not only had I bought two houses ideally located right near the university, I also bought just before the real estate boom," he recalls, noting he bought the duplex for $110,000 in 1987 and sold just two years later for $220,000 – twice what he'd originally paid. The huge return on investment would later be used, in part, to buy his own home and as seed money to fund the start-up of his own company.

After three years with 3M, Mr. Lindsay was ready to take on another challenging opportunity. He found that opportunity in Oakville – and it marked his first, fateful foray into the world of mortgage brokering.

In 1989, he began working as a mortgage broker for Goldmore Financial (now The Mortgage Department), an Oakville-based mortgage broker. That same year, he decided to set down some roots, and he bought a house in Burlington. Lindsay soon discovered that although he was working for a mortgage broker in Oakville, "most of my clients were in Hamilton, so I was also being drawn to this city."

"I really like Hamilton," Mr. Lindsay asserts. "It's smaller than Toronto but it still has everything a big city has to offer, and the people are very friendly. It does however need a strong core, a strong nucleus for sustainable growth," he notes.

"I also found the lenders here in Hamilton to be quite approachable. This is a blue-collar town but approaching the size of a metropolis." Mr. Lindsay decided to lay down more Steel City roots, actively seeking out local lenders while also building the bulk of his clientele base in Hamilton.

"I found the winning combination in Hamilton," he

125

explains. "Hamilton offers a good source of approachable private lenders and a sizeable client base of people who need mortgages and turn to us for service and advice."

The transition from broker to broker-owner took place incrementally, over the course of a few years, during which time Lindsay built a solid reputation as a straight-forward broker who worked closely with clients to achieve the best mortgages possible on their behalf.

His growing success was also forged on his willingness to listen closely to what clients were saying concerning both their need for a mortgage and their income and affordability concerns. His approach inevitably resulted in the creation of custom-made mortgages and very satisfied clients.

And his approach attracted a seemingly never-ending series of referrals that continues to this day. In fact, his company owes much of its strong, continued prosperity to referrals based on exemplary past performance.

In 1991, Mr. Lindsay took the plunge and founded his own firm on King Street West in Hamilton, near Queen Street. Starting up Mortgage Financial was not without risk. "It's always a major adjustment to go from something that's relatively secure to something that's new and different," he recalls. "But I knew this was something I wanted to do, something I really had to do and I was prepared to take on the risks of venturing out on my own."

Although Toronto was then, as now, the main financial centre of Ontario and Canada, Lindsay saw in Hamilton, a vibrant city rich in potential.

"In Hamilton, I saw a service-oriented opportunity," he recalls. "I got in this business when it was relatively young so I could build on my modest investment in my company."

"Back in 1991, my company was very small," he recalls. "It was just myself and one other broker – but we were ready to grow from there."

Mr. Lindsay would come to outgrow that first location

and he moved, in 1998, to his current headquarters on Ray Street, just a few blocks away from the original offices. He owns the stately office building on Ray Street South – purchased for $171,000 – that was converted from a 130-year-old mansion a short walk from the Scottish Rite.

"That year, 1998, was really a very tough year," Mr. Lindsay recalls, shaking his head. "I owed $50,000 in taxes at that point, plus I had just put $50,000 down on the Ray Street building and had a mortgage for the rest," he adds. "My wife had just had twins and we bought a van. Altogether, it was a larger debt-load than I'd ever experienced and I had to work many long, hard hours to generate sufficient income to keep it all under control."

Weathering that financial situation gave the young mortgage broker some first-hand sympathy for what many people encounter when they take on the heady costs associated with a mortgage, other debts and, of course, the never-ending costs of raising a family. Simply put, Lindsay also came to appreciate, in 1998, what it means to be stretched to max.

"That was the most risk I've ever taken on in my life," he acknowledges with raised eyebrows. "But it motivated me to succeed," he adds. "I know what our clients go through. I've been there. I know what it's like to wonder if you'll qualify for a mortgage and what it's like to have to make those payments."

The experience would also have a profound affect on Mr. Lindsay. "To stay on top of it all, I consolidated all my debts into a better package and started working away at paying it down," he explains. "But it was necessary at that time to take on this debt and the business had to rank high on the priority list. It had to be done – so I did it. I now pay as I go, all the time, as much as humanly possible," Lindsay asserts. "And I try to take on very little debt. In fact, I make a real effort to keep my fixed costs and debt to a minimum."

In running Mortgage Financial, he's assisted by his

brother Mike Lindsay and a dedicated support staff. Also helping drive Mortgage Financial to new heights is a team of broker-agents. "I really like our office atmosphere," Mr. Lindsay acknowledges with a grin. "They're a great group and we enjoy bouncing ideas off each other. It's impressive when I think that we have a large group of people all helping each other out."

While he still handles some deals directly, Mr. Lindsay is also heavily involved in running his office, handling payroll and provide problem-solving and direction skills to the company.

"To a certain extent, I depend on my broker-agents to build business volume," he explains. "But I also still enjoy arranging mortgages myself whenever the opportunity presents itself," Mr. Lindsay adds.

"Having the Kronas Group – one of the largest private lenders in the Hamilton area – right in our building is also a big benefit," he notes. "Getting financing for a mortgage is often as simple as going upstairs in this building for a visit with someone from the Kronas Group."

Mr. Lindsay believes much of his firm's success is owed to its prominence in the Hamilton market and its ability to arrange an array of mortgages.

"Our business volume helps us achieve successful placement of mortgages at more than competitive rates," he notes, "and I think that, more than anything else, has helped us to grow, year by year. I anticipate growth continuing in the 30 per cent range, but I'd be happy with even half of that." And Mr. Lindsay still clearly enjoys his hands-on approach to brokering mortgages. "We do all the negotiating and shopping around for rates on the client's behalf," he says, adding "in most cases, most of shopping is done in my head because I know which lenders to use and where to place a given mortgage."

The shopping is also done in advance of meeting with

clients. By the time an actual meeting between customer and broker takes place, the Mortgage Financial representative usually has in place a short list of advantageous mortgage options for the client to choose from. Clients also benefit from Mr. Lindsay's access to a large pool of lenders, the negotiating clout his volume of business gives him with the banks and his industry savvy and his ability to negotiate a win-win deal for the customer and lender.

"We can custom tailor a mortgage to the customer's needs right off the bat because we have so many lenders and mortgage products to choose from," he notes.

To tailor a mortgage to the client's needs, Mr. Lindsay or one of his broker-agents will sit down with the customer and determine what their income levels are, how much mortgage they can afford to carry, what payment schedules are best-suited for them, how determined they are to pay off the mortgage and what other options are worth considering.

For example, mortgage options can include the length of amortization – whether the total mortgage life span runs 10, 15, 20 or 25 years. A shorter amortization means the mortgage is paid off entirely much more quickly, but the weekly or monthly payments are much higher than they would be with a longer amortization period. Regardless of the amortization, weekly payments (or payments every two weeks) are often recommended as they effectively translate into an extra monthly payment each year, which in turn means the mortgage is being reduced a little more quickly and conveniently.

Mortgage options can include a number of variations in the length of the term – whether one wants to go six months, one year, two years, three years or five years before renewing the mortgage. The borrower may also want to knock down the size of the mortgage by having extra payment privileges that allow for larger payments or a lump sum payment or both during the mortgage term.

A down payment of 25 per cent or more of the purchase price will not only dramatically reduce the size of the resulting mortgage, it will also save the borrower costs of getting the mortgage insured by Canada Mortgage and Housing Corporation. CMHC insurance – for high leverage loans of more than 75 per cent of the purchase price – often adds several thousand dollars to the mortgage.

There are still also mortgage variations, including fixed rates that lock you in at a set interest rate for the mortgage term, and variable rates, which are tied to market interest rates and follow those rates up or down.

Variable rates are often considered attractive to borrowers if they anticipate rates remaining low or falling. But if rates rise, the borrower pays the higher rate.

Fixed rates are sometimes a little more costly, but they provide the stability of certainty over the level of interest rate the borrower will pay.

Mr. Lindsay notes his ability to draw on a number of lenders means he can offer just about any mortgage package combination imaginable. "If you, as an individual, are still limiting yourself to one lending institution, you pretty much have to take what you can get – and that's often not the greatest deal that's out there in the marketplace," he observes.

Mr. Lindsay also derives a considerable sense of satisfaction in helping clients obtain the mortgage that's best for them. "It's a great feeling when we're able to get someone a terrific interest rate and terms," he says. "And it's also a great feeling when someone who figured they'd never be able to buy a house is able to get a mortgage through us and achieve the dream of home ownership."

Contact information for Mortgage Financial Corp:
12 Ray Street South, Hamilton, Ontario. L8P 3V2
(905) 529-2521. Toll Free Line: 1-866-604-8860.
Fax: (905) 525-9701. Ken Lindsay: ken@mfco.ca

Dr. Roland Estrabillo:
Dental services for an expanding community

Just as the financial services sector has flourished with the airport's proven ability to attract more people into the Hamilton region, so too has the medical sector grown with physical expansions and rising patient loads.

Dr. Roland Estrabillo is a case in point: Faced with a burgeoning Hamilton area population, the 46-year-old dentist first expanded his practice and building on Hamilton Mountain, and then further increased his practice with addition of a second building, this one a sprawling facility, in Hamilton's Ancaster community just a short drive from Hamilton International.

"The airport has had an indirect impact on dental profession," Dr. Estrabillo notes. "A lot of people are moving into our community – many of them coming from other countries – and the Hamilton area population is growing as a result, along with the need for dental services."

Dr. Estrabillo, who originally hails from the Philippines has also established a charitable free clinic, as part of the Global Smiles International agency he started, that is providing dental care to Hamilton's impoverished citizens who cannot afford such services. One Saturday each month, Dr. Estrabillo and volunteers from his staff of around 50 dentists, hygienists, dental assistants and support staff, freely give of their time and dental skills to help treat more than 400 patients at the free clinic annually.

"It's our way of giving back to the community and it's really incredible how generous our people are with their time," he explains in an interview at his Ancaster offices, where the free clinics also take place.

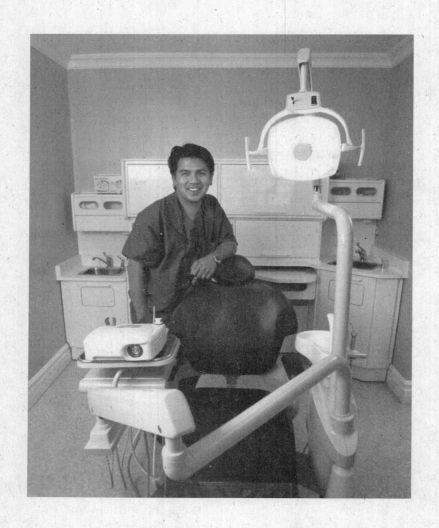

"We see twenty people or more at each clinic and the services we provide range from hundreds to as high as a thousand dollars with all fees waived, he explains."

"We're coming from a place of generosity and many of the patients are very appreciative and grateful for this care," Dr. Estrabillo says of the Global Smiles International free clinics. "It's very satisfying to see the look on the patients' faces and to hear such positive comments."

Follow-up care, also at minimal cost to the patient, is provided at the dental hygiene school Dr. Estrabillo established in the lower level of the Ancaster building. The school, fully registered with the Ontario Ministry of Colleges and Universities and in the process of receiving formal accreditation, has become an important source of dental education and practical field experience.

The Sprawling Ancaster building also houses the dental hygiene training school and a dental lab.

For all of his patients, Dr. Estrabillo employs many of the latest technological advancements to make dental procedures as fast, efficient and comfortable as possible. He's also a life-long student who continues to learn from his mentors: fellow dentists, staff and friends from all walks of life who have helped him overcome problems and achieve new levels of success in his demanding career.

"Success is never something you achieve all by yourself. It's when learn from others and share your own experiences that you improve in the process. And everyone benefits from this type of sharing," he notes.

Dr. Estrabillo's story begins half a world away in the rice paddies of the Philippines. Roland Estrabillo was born Dec. 17, 1960, the youngest of eight children born to Engracio and Virginia Estrabillo. It was, and remains, a close-knit family that prides itself on the success achieved by all family members.

From an early age, the future dentist helped doing

chores at his father's rice paddies and sugar cane fields on a farm on the outskirts of the little town of Magliman, with a population 1,000 farming souls.

"Growing up working class, we didn't have very much," Dr. Estrabillo recollects. "But my dad was very ambitious and we all worked together, as expected, to do the best we could possibly do in the Philippines class system."

In addition to farming, Dr. Estrabillo's hard-driving, entrepreneurial father ran his own trucking business and a hair-cutting enterprise and worked as a labourer at the Clark Air Force Base, the sprawling U.S. military base on the outskirts of the nearby community of San Fernando (population 50,000).

"My dad was very hard-working but he felt he was being passed over for promotions because he only had a Grade 2 education," Dr. Estrabillo recalls. "He wanted a better life for us, so my dad did everything in his power to make sure all of his children had a good education," he adds.

"Dad saved up as much money as he could and he began sending us to university, one after the other."

Dr. Estrabillo says that each child became university-educated in progression of age; they were expected to contribute to the financing of education for siblings following them.

"I guess the one advantage to my being the youngest is that I didn't have to sponsor anyone after me, I only had to consider my own education," Dr. Estrabillo says with a chuckle.

After graduating from high school in San Fernando, Estrabillo studied preparatory medicine and medical technology at Far Eastern University in Manila from 1977 to 1980.

It was then that Dr. Estrabillo was ready to begin a familiar family migration to Canada. His sister Flora, now 65, had been the first in the family to emigrate to North America, settling first in Chicago and then moving to Hamilton to take a nursing position.

Eventually, the entire family would follow, including the parents who live in Hamilton but spend winters in the Philippines.

"My sister really started it all," Dr. Estrabillo notes. "She came to Hamilton because of greener pastures, greater opportunities. She's the reason we're all here."

A teenaged Roland Estrabillo arrived in Canada from the Philippines in 1980. He was 19 and his arrival in The True North, Strong and Free, was the realization of a long-held dream.

"When I got here I just breathed in the air and looked around me and I knew anything was possible – I knew nothing could stop me from accomplishing anything I set out to do," he recollects.

"Every Canadian has the opportunity to pursue anything they want to do. We are so truly fortunate here, it's unbelievable. It really is the land of opportunity."

On arrival, it was found that he was lacking calculus, so he redid Grade 13 at St. Thomas Moore and then enrolled at the University of Toronto where he studied natural sciences for the next two years while pursuing a career in medicine.

Roland Estrabillo continued to pursue his medical studies, working summers and earning scholarships.

He was then ready for the next fateful step.

Roland Estrabillo decided he would apply to the faculties of both medicine and dentistry and was accepted for both.

He turned to a friend, a professor in the faculty of nuclear medicine, who promptly asked the young man if he ever wanted to have a family and lead a normal life.

"I said yes," Dr. Estrabillo recalls, "and he told me to try dentistry, then come back after one year."

Roland Estrabillo took one year of dentistry studies and still wasn't convinced. So he took another "and I knew then that I'd found what I was looking for."

"I'm very grateful for having been steered in this direction and even my own children are very interested in following me and becoming dentists when they grow up. They've seen what dentistry is all about and they know it's a very worthwhile profession."

After Estrabillo graduated in 1987 from the University of Toronto with a degree in dentistry, he returned to Hamilton that same year to set up practice on Upper Wentworth Street, in a little 1,500-square-foot location next to a supermarket in a strip mall opposite Lime Ridge Mall.

As the youthful dentist began building his fledgling practice, he displayed a voracious appetite for information and ideas, boldly seeking out new ways of doing things, new ways of approaching dentistry and life in general.

This openness to new ideas and to learning from the success of others would have a profound and last effect on him.

As Dr. Estrabillo continued to evolve as a successful dentist and explored all that life had to offer, a pivotal moment would occur in 1989 while he was enjoying the splendour of islands in the Pacific Ocean.

The young dentist was wading into a warm water lagoon when a group of boisterous dolphins came splashing towards him, leaping through the water with unbridled joy.

As Dr. Roland Estrabillo stood transfixed in the water off a beach in Hawaii, the dolphins danced into the sheltered cove, chattering excitedly. They seemed to be beckoning the Hamilton dentist to join them.

"They have such a joyful attitude – wouldn't it be nice if you could be as happy as a dolphin in life?" Dr. Estrabillo adds, "and I love their sense of freedom, confidence and happiness."

"It was an experience I'll never forget," he says of the happy encounter.

Inspired by the dolphins, Dr. Estrabillo placed likenesses of their happy images on his business cards and practice literature.

As well, he's decorated the walls of one dental practice location with large illustrations of dolphins at play. He's also infused himself and his staff with a contagious dolphin-like, happy, confident attitude that puts patients at ease and makes trips to the dentist more enjoyable.

"I still love dolphins," Estrabillo admits. "The dolphin's image has become my own private signature – my patients are always bringing me little figurines and pictures of dolphins when they return from travelling. It's nice that people associate me with such a free and happy creature."

That Dr. Estrabillo would learn from dolphins and apply those lessons to his practice isn't surprising: He is determined to keep up in the rapidly evolving field of dentistry.

Dr. Estrabillo believes in lifelong learning and has long selected mentors from dentistry and other fields to give him guidance.

He also mainly uses porcelain, limiting his use of metals to gold and titanium – and only for special applications where porcelain is not the most appropriate material to use. He favours porcelain as it is durable, free of metals, and very natural looking. And he invests in computer equipment; technology, methodologies and materials to ensure his busy practice can treat his many patients fast and efficiently.

For example, although he now regularly makes use of an anaesthesiologist, the I-V sedation certification he earned a few years ago means that he can, if need be, comfortably sedate his patients for longer periods while he performs cosmetic dentistry or full-mouth reconstructive surgery.

It's this constant attention to the needs and concerns

of his patients that have helped this dentist's practice achieve remarkable ongoing growth through a steady stream of referrals.

Back in the early 1990s, while building his practice from scratch, Dr. Estrabillo outgrew his mall location within his first few years of running his dental practice.

In the fall of 1992, Dr. Estrabillo moved his practice to renovated offices at his former home, just a little further north on Upper Wentworth Street.

But it wouldn't be long before he was again feeling cramped. After expanding the number of operating rooms – known as operatories in the dental profession – to seven from four, he soon again found himself short of space.

Although general family dentistry still accounted for 60 per cent of his practice in the mid-1990s, Dr. Estrabillo was concentrating more on full-mouth reconstructive dentistry as a growing, satisfying, part of his work.

And by the late 1990s, Estrabillo was even more heavily involved in personally performing the more complicated dental procedures and "more surgery and less drill-and-fill work," while his practice as a whole continued to perform general dentistry.

"We work as a team – for example, after the orthodontist and periodontist have treated the patient, I perform bridge work, teeth implants, crowns, veneers and cosmetic improvements to teeth," he explains.

"We've cut the time needed for a crown to half an hour from an hour, so the patient is more comfortable."

Dr. Estrabillo now takes three hours instead of seven to perform most full-mouth reconstruction procedures.

He notes this dentistry can improve chewing efficiency, improve the functioning of the jaw, save teeth and "actually make people look younger with whiter, rearranged, straighter teeth which support the mouth better."

By the late 1990s, Estrabillo also had an expanded

patient load of more than 10,000 patients on file.

He then began contemplating moving to larger offices in Hamilton to serve his seemingly endlessly growing practice.

But instead of relocating, he expanded, keeping the Hamilton location while adding the Ancaster location featuring 20,000-square-feet of space and seven operatories. The Ancaster location also houses a dental lab.

Dr. Estrabillo's Ancaster location also features 64 parking spaces, separate offices for course work and a lecture hall.

The two-storey Ancaster building, on Wilson between Jerseyville Road and Halson Avenue, had started construction in 2002, with completion in January 2003.

Both Hamilton locations are needed to keep pace with a burgeoning patient load that has now expanded to more than 12,000 patients on file.

Fuelling this impressive growth are referrals from satisfied patients who appreciate the extra care Estrabillo takes to make visits pleasant and brief.

Also fuelling referrals are the many services he can offer, including laser dentistry, whitening, and implant dentistry. "A lot of people come to us for a whole range of services, including teeth implants – and we like to help them get their mouths back in great shape," Dr. Estrabillo smiles.

Few people can combine the words 'dental' and 'exciting' in one sentence and make it work.

But Dr. Estrabillo is very convincing when he confides: "It's just so exciting to be able to provide all these dental services to our patients – and it's very gratifying when you can help so many people."

Dr. Estrabillo clearly loves dentistry, and he's always looking for new ways of expanding his knowledge and skills in all dental matters.

He frequently works non-stop all day and into the

evening, before heading home. He then makes dinner, takes care of other household chores. Then, from midnight to 2 am, it's his personal time when he reads about dentistry before going to bed to rise the next day at 5 am and do it all again.

Dr. Estrabillo asserts he only needs a few hours sleep. "I only sleep three hours a night – three to five hours is enough for me because I've trained myself to get by on very little sleep and still totally functional," explains the self-confessed workaholic, "and I think three hours is enough sleeping time."

"I do spend a lot time at work," he adds. "But I have a balanced life because I also devote a lot of time to my priorities. My highest priority is my spirituality – the Catholic religion, followed by our health, our family life and then my profession."

"The only thing I don't spend much time on is sleeping," he asserts. "But I feel fine, really good. I don't think I'm suffering from sleep deprivation."

Indeed, while others sleep, Dr. Estrabillo is active and enjoying a full life.

He estimates the wake-time he's gained by cutting back on his sleep will amount to a full 12 years over the course of his lifetime.

"Can you imagine what you can accomplish with 12 extra years?" he asks. "I don't want to waste 12 years of my life on sleep," he adds.

"There isn't enough time in a day right now to do all the things I want to do. But I can't give up sleep completely, so I get a few hours sleep and enjoy the extra time that I'm awake."

Dr. Estrabillo is clearly putting his added time to productive use: In addition to a thriving dental practice, keeping current with the latest dental techniques, lecturing on matters dental and devoting attention to his family, he continues to learn from other successful people,

"I'm still into mentoring," he confirms. "It's a good learning process to talk to people who have achieved success in their lives and learn from them."

And he's grateful for the input, advice and support he's received from his mentors, fellow dentists, staff and friends from all walks of life who have helped him overcome problems and achieve new levels of success in a demanding, time-consuming career.

Dr. Estrabillo directly attributes much of the success of his busy practice to his staff of 40 professionals, including hygienists, restorative hygienists (who can perform fillings work), support staff, and dentist associates. "My staff is great," he says with a grin.

"Without them I couldn't succeed. We do the best job we can - and we try to have fun in the process. We really enjoy our work."

He's also determined to make his office, himself and his entire staff as financially successful as possible.

"Money is a good motivator but after a while it doesn't have the same strong effect as an incentive," Dr. Estrabillo explains. "So it's important to offer praise and to offer other motivations and opportunities to advance in their careers."

The Hamilton dentist also provides his entire staff with the opportunity and ample encouragement to continue increasing their job qualifications and credentials.

"We want our staff to pursue their dreams, to go for higher education and take advantage of the opportunities they have to improve themselves and make this an even better practice," he explains.

As his practice continues to grow, Dr. Estrabillo sees further good times ahead for his entire staff.

"Every year we're experiencing phenomenal growth – the excitement level of the staff is just unbelievable," he exclaims.

"I see a very bright future for our staff, our patients, everyone involved. Life is a great learning experience – and we're always learning new ways to do what we do a little better."

Contact Information for Dr. Roland Estrabillo:
Phone: 905-387-2600 or 905-304-6300 Fax: 905-304-4768
Address: Hamilton location: 860 Upper Wentworth Street, Hamilton, Ontario, L9A 4W4.
Address: Ancaster location: 201 Wilson Street, Ancaster, Ontario. Email: dr.rolandestrabillo@drestrabillo.com

Epilogue

In conversation, Latinos frequently use the term destino. Call it fate, if you like, or simply destiny, a more direct translation.

In any event, I couldn't help but think of that term when I was completing this book.

Earlier, I had written about the history of the air show in Hamilton, and how it brought back a flood of memories.

So it came as a rather illuminating coincidence that, just as I was putting the finishing touches on Flying High, a thunderous boom sounded outside my back door in Brantford, Ontario.

I looked out and there, up in the sky, flying by, was the source of the noise: one of the Canadian Forces Snowbirds, which, one day earlier, had been at Hamilton John C. Munro International Airport (hi).

Officially known as the Canadian Forces 431 Squadron Demonstration Team, the Snowbirds had been in Mount Hope at the Canadian Warplane Heritage Museum to help kick off a book launch, the second edition of A Tradition of Excellence: Canada's Airshow Team Heritage, by retired Lieutenant Colonel Dan Dempsey. And it was their only planned stop in Hamilton in 2007.

And now they were here in Brantford, right behind my house, as I was dotting the I's and crossing the T's on this book.

Too strange to be true? Perhaps. But it sure got me thinking about destino.

So I sat on my deck, contemplating how the stars sometimes align, and realizing that my bird's-eye view near the Grand River gave me an ideal vantage point of other fly-bys: more Snowbirds, but also an Avro Lancaster bomber, an F-16CJ Viper and a B-52 Bomber.

They were all part of the 2007 Brant United Way Air Show, which kicked off the annual United Way fundraising campaign in Brantford. They were rehearsing for the big event and, as fate would have it, their route took a direct right-to-left path across the sky behind my backyard.

What goes around, comes around.

Destino indeed.

Manor House Publishing Inc.
www.manor-house.biz 905-648-2193